Essential
Kenya

by Paul Murphy

PASSPORT BOOKS
NTC/Contemporary Publishing Group

Above: *Kikuyu tribal costume*

Page 1: *elephants at Amboseli*

Page 5a: *Masai women*

Page15a: *lion cub, Masai Mara National Reserve*

Page 27a: *zebras*
27b: *acrobat in Mombasa hotel*

Page 91a: *souvenirs for sale at Nairobi market*
91b: *Giriama women*

Page 117a: *relaxing on Diani Beach*
117b:*security guard, Nairobi*

Published by Passport Books, a division of NTC/ Contemporary Publishing Group, Inc. 4255 West Touhy Avenue, Lincolnwood (Chicago), Illinois 60646–1975 U.S.A.

Copyright © The Automobile Association 1998
Maps © The Automobile Association 1998
Reprinted Oct 1998

The contents of this publication are believed correct at the time of printing. Nevertheless, the publishers cannot accept responsibility for errors or omissions, nor for changes in details given. We are always grateful to readers who let us know of any errors or omissions they come across, and future printings will be updated accordingly.

Published by Passport Books in conjunction with The Automobile Association of Great Britain.

Written by Paul Murphy

Library of Congress Catalog Card Number: 97-76432
ISBN 0–8442–0117–0

Color separation: BTB Digital Imaging, Whitchurch, Hampshire

Printed and bound in Italy by Printer Trento srl

The weather chart on **page 118** of this book is calibrated in °C. For conversion to °F simply use the following formula:
$$°F = 1.8 \times °C + 32$$

Contents

About this Book

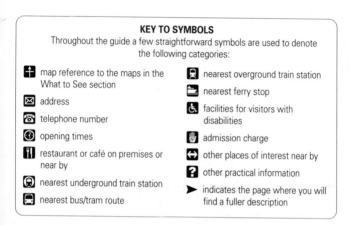
Essential *Kenya* is divided into five sections to cover the most important aspects of your visit to Kenya.

Viewing Kenya pages 5–14
An introduction to Kenya by the author
  Kenya's Features
  Essence of Kenya
  The Shaping of Kenya
  Peace and Quiet
  Kenya's Famous

Top Ten pages 15–26
The author's choice of the Top Ten places to see in Kenya, each with practical information.

What to See pages 27–90
The five main areas of Kenya, each with its own brief introduction and an alphabetical listing of the main attractions
  Practical information
  Snippets of 'Did You Know…' information
  4 suggested walks
  3 suggested tours
  4 features

Where To… pages 91–116
Detailed listings of the best places to eat, stay, shop, take the children and be entertained.

Practical Matters pages 117–24
A highly visual section containing essential travel information.

Maps
All map references are to the individual maps found in the What to See section of this guide.
For example, Mount Kenya has the reference ➕ 28B3 – indicating the page on which the map is located and the grid square in which the mountain is to be found. A list of the maps that have been used in this travel guide can be found in the index.

Prices
Where appropriate, an indication of the cost of an establishment is given by **£** signs:
£££ denotes higher prices, **££** denotes average prices, while **£** denotes lower charges.

Star Ratings
Most of the places described in this book have been given a separate rating:
✪✪✪ Do not miss
✪✪ Highly recommended
✪ Worth seeing

Viewing
Kenya

Paul Murphy's Kenya

Taking Precautions
Before you go anywhere outside your hotel, including the beach, you must take precautions. Leave your camera for the game parks and guided excursions only, take off your watch and any ostentatious jewellery and carry no bags. Keep a little bit of change accessible in your pockets and any other money hidden somewhere about your person.

For most travellers Kenya is quite simply the very best of Africa. Here you will find some of the finest game parks in the world, magnificent mountain and valley scenery, and white-sand beaches fringed with coral reefs.

Accommodation is of the highest standard, and security, certainly within the lodges and game parks, is virtually guaranteed. Yet, just the other side of the road from your 5-star creature comforts you will find communities who live in thatched huts, who have never known electricity and who think nothing of walking several kilometres each day to collect firewood and water. One of Africa's most enduring everyday images is of women dressed in vividly coloured *kangas* walking along the side of dusty red tracks with baskets and water containers balanced on their heads.

Viewing herds of beautiful creatures such as Grevy's zebra is a highlight of any visit

A Kenyan holiday can be a little too easy. A week by the ocean followed by a week on safari is more likely to broaden your backside than your mind. There is more to Kenya than beach and bush, but if you want to see it you'll have to break free from your hotel cocoon. Take a chance, hire a local guide and see what lays out there. See the people, see their markets, see some sights off the beaten track – in short, discover a little bit of the real Kenya.

Kenya's Features

Geographical Information
• **Area**: Kenya covers nearly 600,000sq km, slightly bigger than France, slightly smaller than Texas. However, the north and northeast are either uninhabited or sparsely habited desert.
• **Highs and lows**: snow-capped Mount Kenya at 5,199m; the coastline which runs 480km, from the Tanzanian border in the southeast to the Somali border in the northeast.
• **Longest river**: the Tana which runs for 700km.

Economic Factors
Population: over 28 million and rising at nearly 4 per cent per year – one of the highest growth rates in the world. The largest tribe is the Kikuyu (nearly 7 million), living

Boundaries
The (almost) straight line which defines Kenya's southern border was drawn by the British and Germans in 1884. Britain took Kenya, including Mount Kilimanjaro, while Germany took Tanganyika (now Tanzania and Zanzibar). In 1886, however, Kilimanjaro was given by Queen Victoria to her grandson, the German kaiser, and so the line was redrawn – with a slight diversion!

mostly in the Central area and around Nairobi. Next largest is the Luo (4.2 milllon), from Western Kenya.
• **Main income**: tourism, tea, coffee, flowers, sisal (rope-fibre), pineapples.

Picking tea at Kericho, Western Kenya; a fast worker can collect nearly 70kg per day

Climate
• **Wet or dry?** January and February are dry; March to May is wet ('long rains'); June to September is dry; October to December is wet ('short rains'). In the west there is no 'dry season' but the pattern is similar.
• **How Hot?** The coast is always hot (average daytime temperature 27–31°C); temperature elsewhere depends on altitude. Nairobi (1,661m) – average daytime temperature 21–6°C. July/August is Kenya's winter.

Essence of Kenya

Below: *Masai* moran
(warriors) dancing
Bottom: *Masai women
taking a break from their
daily chores*

To most westerners, Kenya is such an assault on the senses that it is difficult to take in its embarrassment of riches. Don't worry if you have only a couple of weeks to visit. The Kenya tourism machine is adept at getting visitors around and with a bit of careful planning a two-week beach-and-safari holiday which starts in Nairobi and ends on the coast can take in some of the more fascinating and thrilling aspects of the country.

THE **10** ESSENTIALS

If you want to get a really complete picture of Kenya, here are the essentials:

• **See the 'Big Five'** – lion, leopard, elephant, rhino and buffalo – but don't worry if the leopards prove elusive.

• **Go snorkelling** on the reef (► 25, 26) – the colours of the fish will astound you.

• **Take a ride** in a hot-air balloon. Floating effortlessly over the Masai Mara is the trip of a lifetime (► 69).

• **See the flamingos** on Lake Bogoria (or wherever they are currently flocking). The sight of thousands of these elegant pink birds en masse is unforgettable.

• **Ride 'the Lunatic Line'** (► 57) from Nairobi to Mombasa. It's one of the slowest, most old-fashioned railway journeys you'll ever make, but with the right companions it's a great experience.

• **Take a dhow trip** (preferably at sundown). Unchanged for centuries, these romantic Arab coastal sailing vessels are a transport of delight.

• **Look into the Rift Valley.** This giant fault line is not only the most awesome geological sight in Africa, but also the Cradle of Mankind (► 10, 23).

• **Spend a night under canvas**. It doesn't matter how luxurious or how basic, it's the proximity to nature that counts.

An impala at Meru National Park

Another hard day's sunbathing on Diani Beach

• **Laze on a white-sand beach** gently lapped by the aquamarine waters of the Indian Ocean. Turtle Bay (Watamu), Shela Beach (Lamu) and Diani Beach are three of the very best.

• **Experience wild Kenya** close-up, on foot. You can walk by yourself at Hell's Gate (► 72) and Saiwa Swamp (► 90), or with various specialist tour operators.

The Shaping of Kenya

Above: *Portuguese explorer Vasco da Gama*
Right: *the Omani House, Fort Jesus, Old Mombasa*

2–4 million years BC
Earliest known human existence on earth begins in the Rift Valley, possibly on the shores of Lake Turkana.

2000–1000 BC
Earliest migrant tribes arrive (from Ethiopia), followed by tribes from the Nile region.

500 BC–AD 500
Earliest migration of Bantu tribes from West Africa.

650–800
Arab and Persian trading posts are set up along the coast. Traders settle and intermarry, introducing Islam and creating the Swahili culture and language.

1498–9
Portuguese explorer Vasco da Gama is the first European to arrive, setting up a trading post at Malindi.

1528
The Portuguese sack the capital of Mombasa and the country comes under their rule.

Early 17th century
Samburu and Masai tribes become the last major tribal groupings to arrive in the country.

1696–8
Portuguese settlements are conquered by the Omanis.

1729
The Portuguese lose Fort Jesus and finally surrender the country to Oman.

1873
An Omani-British treaty bans Kenya's lucrative export of slaves.

1895
The British Government declares East Africa (Uganda and Kenya) a Protectorate.

1896–1901
The East Africa/Uganda Railway (the 'Lunatic Line') is built from Mombasa to Lake Victoria, founding Nairobi en route (in 1899) and opening up the Central Highlands for European development. An army of some 20–30,000 Indian workers is imported to build the line and help run the railway.

1907
Nairobi becomes the capital of the East African Protectorate.

1901–16
Large influx of European (mainly British) settlers.

Coffee and tea are introduced.

1920–3
Following World War I, cheap land is given to British ex-servicemen under the Soldier Settlement Scheme, which doubles the British population to around 9,000.

1946
Jomo Kenyatta becomes the head of the Kenyan African Union party.

1950s
The Mau Mau terror campaign is unleashed by Kikuyu nationalists seeking independence from Britain. A state of emergency is declared in 1952 and its leaders, including Kenyatta, are arrested. In 1954, 30,000 Kikuyu are detained for questioning and 20,000 imprisoned as suspected Mau Mau supporters. In total, some 13,000 Africans and around 100 Europeans are killed during the troubles.

1960
The Lancaster House conference in London paves the way for Kenya's independence (*Uhuru*).

1963
Kenya gains independence with Jomo Kenyatta as first Prime Minister.

1964
Kenya becomes a republic, with Kenyatta as executive president.

1968
A policy of 'Africanisation' is instated. Land bought from white settlers is divided into small-holdings and given to African farmers. Asians leave the country in their thousands.

1978
Kenyatta dies and is succeeded, without election, by Vice-President Moi.

1982
Moi survives an attempted Kenyan Air Force coup. Many people die on the streets of Nairobi in the chaotic bloody aftermath.

1989
A near-worldwide ivory ban is implemented at Kenya's behest and wardens are given shoot-on-sight instructions to combat poaching.

1992
International pressure forces President Moi to hold multi-party

Kenya's elephants, back from the brink of extinction

elections. The opposition, however, is disorganised and fragmented and Moi, with a great deal of political chicanery, is returned to power.

Peace & Quiet

With the notable exceptions of Nairobi and Mombasa, peace and quiet is easy to find anywhere in Kenya. Most visitors tend to flock to a comparatively small number of sites and once away from these honeypots you can find yourself quite alone. However, given the security situation and the inherent dangers of independent travel in the bush, this may not be so easy or appealing as it sounds. The good news is that you can usually get away from the crowds, even in such popular parks as the Masai Mara, Samburu and Tsavo. Indeed, many of the places described in the book take you well away from other people. The following highlights some of these and also looks at other options.

Above: Meru National Park at dusk
Right: the gerenuk, in appearance half-gazelle, half-giraffe

The Rest of Kenya
Much of Eastern Kenya and the whole of the Northeastern Province have effectively been declared out of bounds by Somali bandits. Nevertheless, on the edge of this wasteland, and within easy reach of civilisation, is Meru National Park, where Joy and George Adamson did much of their work (➤ 14). Its jungle-like scenery is beautiful, the game-viewing is good and you'll probably have it all to yourself. Check out the security situation before your visit.

Some of the most awe-inspiring and emptiest landscapes in Kenya lie in the northern Rift Valley, around Lake Turkana. However, this area is for hardened travellers only. You can fly in, but to soak up the atmosphere you should consider joining an overland excursion. Independent travel is discouraged, and may even be forbidden, for very real security reasons.

The Coast
If you are seeking solitude, as a general rule avoid Diani Beach and Malindi. But even here there are many pockets of tranquillity, and the type and location of accommodation within the resort may be of more relevance than the actual resort. Arguably, the best, and certainly one of the quietest, beaches on the coast is Shela Beach on Lamu Island (➤ 41).

The Central Highlands
Aside from the ever-popular Ark and Treetops lodges, the Aberdare National Park is completely untouched by tour operators (➤ 62–3). Mount Kenya is possibly the ultimate away-from-it-all, apart, that is, from your porters and fellow travelling companions (➤ 66).

The Southern and Central Rift Valley
Kenya's most southerly Rift Valley attraction is Lake Magadi, a 120km drive south of Nairobi. If you are not deterred by the ferocious heat – it's one of the hottest places in the country – you'll probably have it all to yourself. The bird-watching is good, often with large numbers of flamingos (check, if possible, before you go). The other Rift Valley lake with plenty of flamingos and few people is Lake Elementeita. Its location, between Lake Nakuru and Lake Naivasha, is both accessible and convenient, and it's much cooler than Magadi.

Kenya's Famous

Jomo Kenyatta (1892–1978)

Jomo Kenyatta, the man who led the nation to Uhuru (freedom)

Jomo Kenyatta took up politics in the early 1920s in Nairobi, acting as a spokesman for African rights. In 1931, he moved to London to further the campaign for his country and stayed for 15 years. He returned a hero and assumed the mantle of nationalist leader. However, in 1952, suspected by the British of organising Mau Mau terror, he was arrested and imprisoned for seven years. On his release he was elected as leader of the KANU party and at Independence in 1963 he became Prime Minister (➤ 11). The following year Kenyatta was made President, a position he held until his death in 1978. Known affectionately as *Mzee* (Father or Elder), he became the Father of the Kenyan nation and one of the heroes of African nationalism. His moderate views and conciliatory approach after Independence made him a distinguished and respected world leader, though the latter years of his administration were clouded by repression and corruption.

The Tribes of Kenya
There are some 40 different tribes in Kenya, of whom the most famous are the Masai and their close relatives, the Samburu. Proud and colourful, they are well known to many tourists, visiting hotels and occasionally opening up part of their homesteads as attractions to show off their culture and sell souvenirs.

George Adamson (1905/6–89) and Joy Adamson (1910–80)

George Adamson was the warden at Meru National Park, and it was here (and at Shaba National Park) that he and his wife Joy hand-reared and returned orphaned lions, leopards and cheetahs back into the wild. Joy immortalised their experiences in her book, *Born Free*, written at Elsamere (➤ 72). The subsequent film catapulted them into the international limelight. Joy was also an accomplished artist, with many works in the National Museum of Kenya (➤ 57). Tragically, both were murdered by poachers – Joy at Meru in 1980, George in Kora in 1989.

Karen Blixen (1885–1962)

Karen Blixen came to Kenya in 1914 to run a coffee farm and stayed until its failure in 1931. She returned to her native Denmark and wrote of her experiences in the classic pastoral account *Out of Africa*. It was published in 1937 under the (male) pen-name of Isak Dinesen, because at the time it was thought that a man's work would sell better than a woman's. The subsequent Oscar-winning film, starring Meryl Streep and Robert Redford, prompted a massive boost in Kenyan tourism (➤ 59).

Top Ten

WILD ANIMALS ARE DANGEROUS

1
The Aberdare Range

28B3

Aberdare Ranges
National Park, PO Box
22, Nyeri

0170-55024

Daily dawn–dusk

Very expensive

*A wild and beautiful mountain range,
the Aberdare Range (or Highlands) includes two
world-famous tree-house game viewing lodges.*

This stark volcanic massif runs roughly north to south for
some 60km between Naivasha and Nyahururu. It peaks at
just below 4,000m with Ol-doinyo Lesatima marking the
third highest spot in all Kenya (after Mount Kenya and
Mount Elgon). Much of the area is designated National
Park.

Sloping down from the mountains are dense tropical
forests and jungle, once a redoubtable hide for Mau Mau
guerillas (► 11) and today still penetrated only by more
adventurous travellers. Four-wheel drive is obligatory if
driving through the park, though the effort is richly
rewarded, with some of Kenya's most pristine scenery and
spectacular waterfalls, including the Gura Falls, at 300m
the highest in the country. Don't expect to see much in
the way of wildlife along this route, however, as the
vegetation is too thick and the animals, unused to human
contact, are too timid (► 64).

By contrast, the Aberdares' European-style high
moorland scenery is familiar to countless numbers of
visitors, either from driving along its northern boundaries
on the scenic B5 Nyahururu–Nyeri road, or more obviously,
heading directly for a night of game viewing at either the
Ark or Treetops lodge hotels (► 62–3).

*The Aberdare Country
Club, a living relic of the
white man's reign in the
highlands*

2
Amboseli National Park

A small but heavily visited park, Amboseli is made famous by Africa's tallest mountain and its great numbers of elephants.

Amboseli is the park that has launched a thousand African travel posters. The classic image of herds of elephants against the backdrop of snow-topped Kilimanjaro ('the Shining Mountain') is known not only to visitors to Kenya but to armchair travellers throughout the world. This apparent Garden of Eden is not without problems, however. No other park in Kenya attracts so many vehicles per square kilometre, and in recent years many of these have ventured off road in search of game, badly degrading the savannah and scrub landscape. The destructive nature of so many elephants in such a relatively small park has also taken its toll.

✠ 28B2

✉ PO Box 18, Namanga

☎ 900-2

🕐 Daily 8–6:30

✋ Very expensive

And then there is the weather. In the early 1990s, flooding almost turned Amboseli into a swamp, while by 1997, drought conditions meant that tour operators were actively discouraging visitors from Amboseli. Ironically, given its recent parched state, Amboseli translates as 'place of water' and the ever-melting snows of Kilimanjaro mean that the park will never dry up, with underground rivers surfacing as swampy springs.

In between weather extremes, game viewing is excellent. Amboseli's main attraction is its elephants; the bulls here have some of the largest tusks in Kenya. Buffalo, zebra, wildebeest, giraffe and impala are also plentiful, and birdlife is varied and interesting.

The heavy mob; a family outing at Amboseli

3
Diani Beach

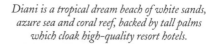

*Diani is a tropical dream beach of white sands,
azure sea and coral reef, backed by tall palms
which cloak high-quality resort hotels.*

31A1

Ali Barbour's Cave
Restaurant (▶ 93)

*Diani Beach, where blue
skies and white sands
mean brown skins for
sun-starved north
Europeans*

This beach is the essence of Kenya's Indian Ocean coastline, and just a photo-glimpse of this paradisaical 10km strand has sold more Kenyan beach holidays than any other place. The seascape, too, plays its part, shared by ageless dhows and outrigger canoes alongside modern glass-bottom boats and state-of-the-art deep-sea fishing launches.

Set back behind the palm trees are large resort hotels with low-level accommodation (chalets and *bandas*). The quietest part of the beach is the residential area to the north, with most activities concentrated on the central and southern stretch. The only blot on this near-perfect landscape are the hustlers ('beach boys'), who are particularly tiresome here.

Inevitably, the sea is the major attraction, with 'goggling' (snorkelling) trips to the reef, windsurfing, deep-sea fishing and scuba-diving the principal activities. Swimming in the late afternoon is not so pleasant when the seaweed comes floating in.

Back on land is a new 18-hole golf course, designed to a high standard and open to the general public. The more enterprising accommodation also offers walking tours of the Jadini Forest, the beautiful hinterland cut off from the beach by the road and now sadly decimated by tourist development. In the small pockets of primeval forest which survive are colobus and vervet monkeys, many species of birds, and bush-babies, whose plaintive cries are a memorable feature of the night.

4
Lamu Island

A dreamy half-forgotten island, more Arabic than East African, Lamu has one of the world's great beaches.

✠ 29D2

🍴 Restaurants (➤ 94)

Geographical isolation and the efforts of conservationists have combined to ensure that Lamu remains the last bastion of Swahili culture on the Kenyan coast. Virtually undisturbed by modern development, it has changed little in appearance since the late 19th century when Omanis and Yemenis were the dominant peoples. The island last gained fame in the 1960s as one of the great hippy hang-outs, and though these travellers have long gone, a mystique still attaches to the island.

The bus journey from Malindi is not recommended (for comfort or security reasons), which means flying into Manda Island, followed by a 10-minute dhow ride to the island and town of Lamu. First impressions – flyblown and dusty – are not encouraging. And as you step back into the

Despite its warlike fort, Lamu is a bastion of peace and quiet

tiny labyrinth of little white boxes that is Lamu town, buildings crumble, drainage overflows and rubbish is strewn liberally. The only outward signs of wealth are the intricately carved wooden doorways for which the island is famous. Fortunately, external appearances are deceptive and the interiors of the houses are often spotlessly white with cool, plant-filled, Arabic-style courtyards and relaxing roof terraces.

Once you have come to terms with Lamu's scruffy appearance its charm begins to grow. The people are friendly, with little of the hassle found elsewhere in Kenya, the alleyways are dotted with interesting little shops and workshops caught in a time warp, and the atmosphere is so relaxed, it's almost soporific. Moreover, there is no 'tourist curfew' here – it's generally quite safe to walk even the darkest alleys by night.

Lamu's *tour de force* lies a short walk or dhow ride from town; Shela Beach, the most spectacular golden sands in all Kenya (➤ 41).

5
Masai Mara National Reserve

✚ 46A2

✉ PO Box 60, Narok

☎ (No tel)

🕐 Daily dawn–dusk

🖐 Very expensive

Kenya's most famous park offers scenery, accommodation and game viewing straight from Out of Africa.

The Masai Mara is the northern end of the Serengeti National Park (which lies in Tanzania) and is the most popular of all Kenya's game parks, with the largest numbers of game and visitors. However, with an area of over 1,500sq km, the Mara (as it is commonly called) is also one of the biggest parks and it is comparatively easy to get away from the crowds.

The busiest area is the southeast corner, where the Nairobi road enters the park. Game viewing is generally held to be better in the northwest, where there is more underground water, as well as the Mara River.

You'll need long lenses and plenty of film on safari

The landscape is mostly savannah, with huge dramatic skies, and game viewing is excellent all year round. You will see prides of lions (there are around 22 families here), elephants (which number around 3,000), buffaloes, giraffes and large numbers of other grazers, including zebra, wildebeest, hartebeest and topi (the latter is a distinctive antelope found only here in Kenya). Other animals frequently seen are the park's 40 or so black rhinos, and the 60 to 70 cheetahs which live in and around the park fringes. Leopards are even more numerous, but elusive. The Mara River is one of the best places in Kenya to see crocodiles and hippos.

Game drives aside, the most popular activity in the Mara is hot-air ballooning (➤ 69); to take a flight during the annual migration (➤ 116) is the ultimate Mara experience.

Where wildebeest and zebra gather, lions are never far behind

6
Mount Kenya

Kenya's greatest mountain dominates the central region and is a fascinating place for walkers, climbers and naturalists.

The sacred mountain – brooding, omnipresent and generally swathed in clouds

✚ 28B3

✉ Mount Kenya National Park, PO Box 69, Naro Moru

☎ 0171-2383

🕐 Daily dawn–dusk

✋ Expensive

At 5,199m, Mount Kenya is the country's highest peak and Africa's second highest mountain, after Mount Kilimanjaro. The first European to see Mount Kenya was a German missionary, Johann Krapf, in 1849. His reports of snow-capped peaks astride the Equator were ridiculed, and it was not until 1833, when the Scottish explorer Joseph Thomson confirmed his story, that the western world conceded its existence. The first European to reach the top was Sir Halford Mackinder in 1899.

Mount Kenya is a volcanic cone and last erupted some 2 million years ago; its highest peaks Batian (the summit) and Nelion, and Lenana, just below, are volcanic plugs. Around Batian, glaciers have carved out deep scenic valleys and tarns which make the ascent of the mountain an unforgettable experience (► 66). If you are fortunate enough to make the climb, you will understand why the Kikuyu and Masai tribes regard Mount Kenya as the home of their Supreme Being, *Ngai*.

For lazy mortals, the most comfortable place from which to view the mountain is the Mount Kenya Safari Club (► 65). Beware: Mount Kenya is shrouded in mist and clouds at most times and reveals her peaks only briefly at dawn and dusk.

The area around the mountain is a National Park, and on the upper slopes the forest belts are host to many different animals and plants, with at least 11 unique types of vegetation.

7

The Rift Valley

Kenya's most spectacular geological phenomenon is also host to one of nature's brightest birdlife gatherings.

✚ 28A2

The Rift Valley, or Great Rift Valley (as it is sometimes called), is a huge fault in the earth's surface, created around 20 million years ago by a series of cataclysmic volcanic events. The resulting Afro-Arabian rift system stretches right across Africa for around 6,000km, from Mozambique to Jordan. Only a fraction of this lies within Kenya but here it is at its narrowest point – around 45km across between the Mau Escarpment and the Aberdares. Consequently, Kenya is the best place in Africa to view the Rift as a valley.

The most obvious viewpoints are those along the roadside heading north on the A104 from Nairobi, close to Nakuru. Down in the valley itself, and clearly visible from these viewpoints, is Mount Longonot. A walk around its crater rim (➤ 78) also offers marvellous views. Arguably, the best roadside views are from the western side of the valley, on the C51, just below Iten (➤ 69). This road cuts across the spectacular Kerio Valley and drops rapidly 1,000m down to Marigat, near Lake Baringo. Other Rift viewpoints include the Ngong Hills (➤ 59), and the window of any light aircraft flying between Nairobi and the Masai Mara.

The other unmissable feature of the Rift Valley in Kenya is the huge flocks of flamingos on its lakes (➤ 74).

Looking down from the Nyambeni Hills, near Meru

8
Samburu Region

➕ 28B3

✉ PO Box 53, Maralal

☎ 0368-2053, 0368-2412

🕐 Daily dawn–dusk

✋ Samburu/Buffalo
Springs (joint admission)
very expensive; Shaba
expensive

*Adventure into the northern wilds to this dry
and dramatic landscape with unusual
variations of wildlife.*

For most visitors to Kenya, Samburu or Shaba is the north-ernmost extent of their safari. At Isiolo, tarmac roads and cultivated green lands end and the wild dusty tracts of the Northern Frontier District begin. This sense of isolation and contrast is a large part of the region's appeal.

The Samburu National Reserve adjoins Buffalo Springs National Reserve and immediately east of here is Shaba National Reserve. Together they form one of Kenya's most interesting game viewing areas, with many animals that are exclusive to or only commonly seen in the north. Grevy's zebra is distinguished from its common cousin by much narrower stripes, while the reticulated giraffe sports a distinctive, dark crazy-paved jigsaw pattern.

Samburu's most unusual resident is the gerenuk, a long-necked gazelle which stands on its hind legs to feed on the higher leaves of bushes. Other notable animals are the beisa oryx and the eland (➤ 50). Predators include cheetahs, leopards (baited at two Samburu lodges) and a small number of lions. Elephants are common in Samburu, though rhinos have sadly been wiped out.

Samburu and Shaba are very dry, but running through both parks is the Ewaso Ngiro (Black River), home to crocodiles and hippos. Herds of buffalo also come down to the shallows to cool off. Distant hills and rocky outcrops make a dramatic backdrop.

*The world's fastest land
animal, the cheetah is
also one of Kenya's most
graceful creatures*

9
Wasini Island & Kisite-Mpunguti Marine National Park

Visit Kenya's finest reef, swim in your own personal 'aquarium' and have a lunch fit for King Neptune on this unspoilt desert island.

Set at the southernmost point of Kenya's coastline, the Kisite Marine National Park (the Mpunguti suffix is usually dropped) is the country's most colourful coral garden. Some 45 varieties of coral have been identified and over 250 types of fish come here to feed in an ever-changing kaleidoscopic feast of colour and movement. Because of its location, between 4 and 8km out to sea, and the fact that it is deep enough to avoid damage from clumsy flippers and anchors, the reef here is in a far better state than comparable reefs to the north.

 31A1

 Wasini Island Restaurant & Kisite Marine Park Dhow Tours, booking office at Jadini Beach Hotel, Diani Beach

0127-2331 or book through your travel agent

Moderate

Access is by boat from Shimoni (▶ 45) on the mainland, where a small flotilla awaits the daily visitors who come to 'goggle' (snorkel) and dive here. You can hire a boat independently, but by far the most popular excursion is the combined Wasini Island Restaurant/Kisite Dhow tour. Guests are collected from their coastal hotels and taken to Shimoni where they board traditional large dhows for the 60-minute journey to the reef by motor and sail. Dolphins swim in these waters and frequently follow the dhows.

After an hour's snorkelling (or diving) a magnificent seafood lunch, with the sand between your toes and *makuti* above your head (▶ 95), is taken on Wasini Island. This is a beautiful, small, undeveloped hideaway with a fascinating dry petrified coral garden to visit. Only at high spring tides does the sea enter this weird maze of peculiar-shaped standing stones.

Fishing boat waiting for the tide to turn off Wasini Island

10
Watamu

Wonderful snorkelling is easily accessible from one of Kenya's most beautiful and hassle-free beaches.

The Malindi and Watamu Marine Park was Kenya's first protected marine park, designated in 1968, and its coral reefs are home to over 140 species of hard and soft coral. Now Watamu is a Marine Park in its own right, and because it is less visited than its popular neighbour its reef is still in very good condition. The snorkelling here is excellent, virtually on a par with Kisite (► 25), and much more accessible in every sense.

Watamu Marine Park also encompasses the mangrove forests of Mida Creek, where young coral grows naturally before the tide takes it out to join on to the main reef. Divers should enquire about a trip to Tewa Caves, near the mouth of the creek, where giant groupers hang almost motionless in the water. These behemoths can weigh up to almost 400kg and measure 2m long, but are completely harmless.

Watamu's beaches are some of the most idyllic spots on the whole Kenyan coast with three glorious bays – Watamu Bay, Blue Lagoon and Turtle Bay, each a perfect crescent of soft white sand. Turtle Bay is particularly attractive, its shallow turquoise and azure waters dotted with small coral islets that you can swim to or walk to at low tide. And best of all, as far as many visitors are concerned, is the lack of hassle from 'beach boys' here.

Watamu is also the focus for sea sports on this section of the coast, with Hemingways (► 101) and Ocean Sports leading the way (► 69). Both establishments also offer snorkelling trips.

Enjoying a relaxing day on the beach at Turtle Bay

What To See

Hiring a catamaran at Nyali Beach, north of Mombasa

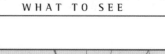

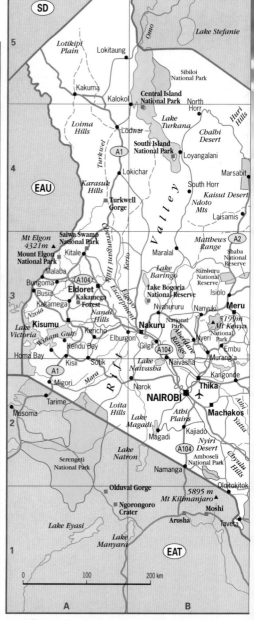

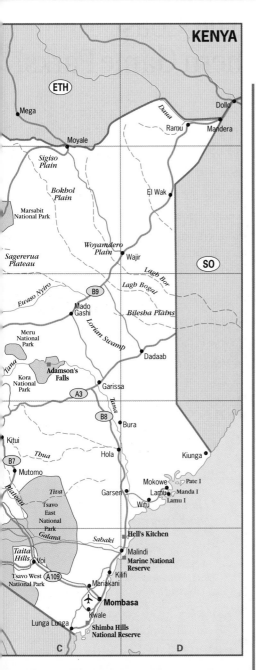

KENYA

ETH

Mega

Daua

Dollo

Moyale
Ramu
Mandera

Sigiso Plain

Bokbol Plain

El Wak

Marsabit National Park

Sagererua Plateau

Woyamdero Plain
Wajir

SO

Ewaso Nyiro

Lagh Bor

Lagh Bogal

B9

Mado Gashi

Lorian Swamp

Bilesha Plains

Meru National Park

Tana

Adamson's Falls

Kora National Park

Dadaab

Garissa

A3

Tana

B8

Bura

Kitui

Thua

Hola

Kiunga

B7

Mutomo

Tiva

Mokowe

Pate I

Plateau

Garsen

Lamu

Manda I

Tsavo East National Park

Witu

Lamu I

Galana

Sabaki

Hell's Kitchen

Taita Hills

Voi

Malindi

Tsavo West National Park

A109

Marine National Reserve

Mariakani

Kilifi

✈ **Mombasa**

Kwale

Lunga Lunga

Shimba Hills National Reserve

C

D

A woman's work is never done in Kenya; fully laden Masai girl

The Coast
(& Southern Game Parks)

The coast is the country's most popular area, and together with its hinterland of superb game parks is all that many visitors see, and indeed require of Kenya. The glorious palm-fringed Indian Ocean beaches, where exotic dhows offer romantic adventure and the coral reefs invite visitors into a whole new underwater world, are clearly the main draw.

Those in search of local culture won't be disappointed either. Parts of the shoreline may be developed, but the coastal villages are still Kenya in the raw. Swahili ruins dot the coast while the port of Mombasa, modern and vibrant, retains exotic and colonial vestiges.

'Haraka Haraka;
haina Baraka.'

OLD SWAHILI PROVERB
Literal translation:
'Haste, haste; there's no
blessing in it.'
Vernacular translation:
'Don't do today what you can put
off until tomorrow.'

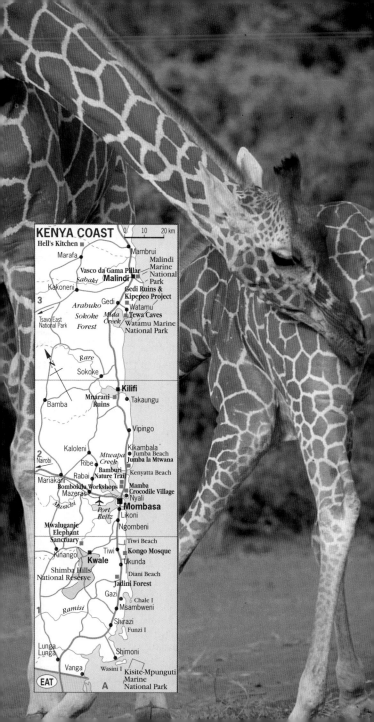

KENYA COAST

Hell's Kitchen
Marafa
Mambrui
Vasco da Gama Pillar
Malindi
Malindi Marine National Park
Sabaki
Kakoneni
Gedi Ruins & Kipepeo Project
Arabuko Gedi
Watamu
Sokoke Mida Creek
Tewa Caves
Forest
Watamu Marine National Park
Tsavo East National Park
3
Rare
Sokoke
Kilifi
Mnarani Ruins
Takaungu
Bamba
Vipingo
Kaloleni
Kikambala
Mtwapa Creek
Jumba Beach
Jumba la Mtwana
Nairobi
Ribe
Bamburi Nature Trail
Kenyatta Beach
2
Rabai
Mariakani
Mamba Crocodile Village
Bombolulu Workshops
Nyali
Mazeras
Mwachi
Port Reitz
Mombasa
Likoni
Ngombeni
Mwaluganje Elephant Sanctuary
Tiwi Beach
Kinango
Tiwi
Kongo Mosque
Kwale
Ukunda
Shimba Hills National Reserve
Diani Beach
Jadini Forest
Gazi
1
Ramisi
Chale I
Msambweni
Shirazi
Funzi I
Lunga Lunga
Shimoni
Vanga
Wasini I
Kisite-Mpunguti Marine National Park

EAT

0 10 20 km

A

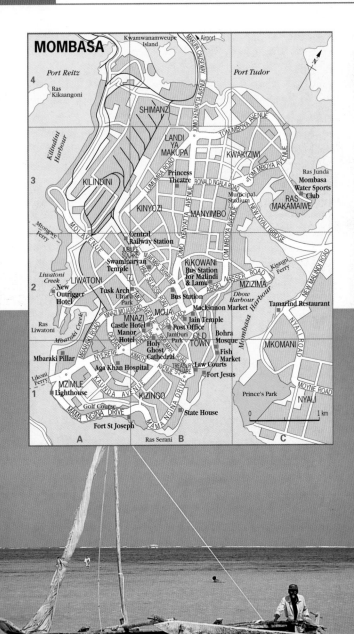

MOMBASA

Kwamwanamweupe Island — Airport

Port Reitz

4

Ras Kikaangoni

SHIMANZI

Port Tudor

Kilindini Harbour

LANDI YA MAKUPA

KWAKIZIWI

3

KILINDINI

Princess Theatre

RONALD NGALA ROAD

Ras Junda

Mombasa Water Sports Club

RAS MAKAMAIWE

KINYOZI

MANYIMBO

Municipal Stadium

NEW NYALI BRIDGE

Mtongwe Ferry

Central Railway Station

JUBILEE SQUARE

Swaminaryan Temple

KIKOWANI

Bus Station for Malindi & Lamu

Kisauni Ferry

NASSER ROAD

2

Liwatoni Creek

LIWATONI

Tusk Arch

Uhuru Park

Bus Station

MZIZIMA

Dhow Harbour

Mombasa Harbour

New Outrigger Hotel

Mackinnon Market

Tamarind Restaurant

Ras Liwatoni

Mbaraki Creek

MNAZI

MOJA

Jain Temple

Jamhuri Park

Post Office

Castle Hotel Manor Hotel

DIGO ROAD

Holy Ghost Cathedral

OLD TOWN

Bohra Mosque

MKOMANI

Mbaraki Pillar

NYERERE

TREASURY SQUARE

Fish Market

NYALI ROAD

Likoni Ferry

Aga Khan Hospital

AVENUE SQUARE

Law Courts

MOYNE ROAD

1

MZIMLE

Lighthouse

KAUNDA AVENUE

KIZINGO

Fort Jesus

Prince's Park

NYALI

Golf Course

MAMA NGINA DRIVE

State House

0   1 km

Fort St Joseph

Ras Serani

A   **B**   **C**

Mombasa

The former capital of Kenya and still one of Africa's major ports, Mombasa is hot, dirty, noisy and colourful. For many visitors the journey from the international airport to the coastal hotels provides quite a culture shock. The city offers few obvious architectural or historical sights, but is still worth a visit for its exuberant atmosphere and bustling street life.

Mombasa enjoyed its golden age in medieval times, with its superb natural harbour and eastward aspect enabling a flourishing trade with Persia, China and India. In 1498, the Portuguese arrived and sacked the city. They stayed, on and off, for the next two centuries, until they were finally driven out by the Omanis, who imparted much of today's Arab atmosphere to the city. The Omanis also brought a second flourish of wealth to Mombasa during the 18th and 19th centuries with slave trading. This ceased in 1873 with the British–Omani treaty, and by the end of the century the city was under British rule. In 1907, it ceded its capital status to Nairobi.

Mombasa is still largely confined to its 15sq km island and divides into three main parts – port, modern city centre and old town. Beaches lie north and south, a short drive through crowded, sprawling, shanty-town suburbs. Today, only the old town holds anything of tourist interest, with visitors coming in to shop and wander the dusty narrow streets leading off from Fort Jesus (➤ 34).

Above: *High Street traders in Mombasa Old Town*

Opposite: *Indian Ocean traders at Diani Beach*

33

Fort Jesus defences.
Between the 17th and
19th centuries the fort
changed hands many
times

What to See in Mombasa

FORT JESUS ✪✪

This sturdy coral-stone fortress is Mombasa's most impressive historical sight. It was built in 1593 by the invading Portuguese and held until 1631 when the local Arabs stormed the fort and massacred the inhabitants. They held it for less than two years, however, until the Portuguese returned. In 1696, the fort was again besieged, and after almost three years the defenders were defeated by plague and starvation.

One of the highlights here is the 18th-century Omani House, whose rooftop gives a good view down over the old town. A small museum houses various Swahili artefacts and objects salvaged from a Portuguese frigate wrecked in the harbour below in 1697.

- ➕ 32B1
- ☎ 011-312839
- ⏰ Daily 8:30–6
- 🍴 Café (Swahili food) on premises (£)
- 💷 Cheap
- ↔ Old Town (➤ 35)
- ❓ Unofficial guides available (cheap); guidebook from the kiosk. Sound and light/dinner show held weekly (☎ 011-472213 or 011-471895) (➤ 113)

MAMA NGINA DRIVE/LIKONI FERRY ✪

Skirting the southern end of the island, Mama Ngina Drive offers fine sea views and links the old town with the Likoni Ferry. At rush hour, the great surge of humanity as it leaves the island aboard the ferry is the most arresting sight in Mombasa. This is also a good point to watch some of the giant tankers heaving into and out of the port of Mombasa.

If you are travelling to Diani Beach, then you have little option but to use the Likoni Ferry.

- ➕ 32A1
- 🚢 Ferry is a 45-minute walk or a few minutes by car from the Old Town (➤ 35)

TUSK ARCH ✪

Mombasa's most famous landmark, two pairs of crossed tusks, was constructed across Moi Avenue (the centre of the new town) to celebrate the coronation of Queen Elizabeth II in 1953. Impressive from afar, close-up they turn out to be riveted sheets of thin rolled metal.

- ➕ 32B2
- ℹ Mombasa tourist information office very close to arch

A Walk Around Mombasa Old Town

This walk takes you through the narrow streets of the old town.

Directly opposite Fort Jesus (➤ 34), fork right into Mbarak Hinawy Road.

Look for the tiered balconies and fine plasterwork on the upper stories of the houses. On the left is the Mandhry Mosque. Founded in 1570, it is Mombasa's oldest mosque still in use. Opposite is a small well used for ritual ablutions.

A few yards further on the left is Government Square. To the right is the old Dhow Harbour and port (small entrance charge to port).

This was once the main harbour for East Africa, handling hundreds of trading ships.

Leave the port. On the right is the Bohra Mosque.

If you are with a guide you can climb the tower's 95 steps and enjoy a splendid view over the tin-corrugated and red-tiled roofs of the old town (charge 200Ksh).

Continue on, turn right on to Ndia Kuu and right again to the Leven Steps (not recommended without a guide).

Named after HMS *Leven*, these steps were built by a British naval officer who became governor of Mombasa. They offer a fine view across the harbour. There is also a stone bath here sunk back into the wall. Legend has it that this was a favoured bathing place of the old Arab slave masters and that the remains of the two boats below (one is sunk deep into the sands) are old slaving vessels.

Return to Ndia Kuu from where Fort Jesus is a short straight walk.

Look up at the ornately carved doors and balconies of several of the houses along here (note Nos 28, 33 and 34 in particular) and browse in the 'curio' shops which are found along the way.

Look out for pretty balconies with all the trimmings

Distance
2–3km

Time
1 hour

Start/end point
Fort Jesus
 32B1
An accompanying guide (available from Fort Jesus) is necessary to climb the Bohra Mosque and is advisable if you want to go to the Leven Steps

Lunch
Fort Jesus (£)

What to See on the Coast

ARABUKO SOKOKE FOREST ✪

Covering an area of 417sq km, this is the largest surviving coastal tropical forest in East Africa and bird enthusiasts rate the Arabuko Sokoke alongside the Kakamega Forest (➤ 84) as the most important reserve in Kenya. It boasts several rare endemic species, but spotting these is often very difficult, particularly for the casual visitor. The park is also proud of its numerous owl and butterfly species and its rare golden-rumped elephant shrew. Take a detailed map if you venture in along the cool, inviting forest trails – it's easy to lose your way.

BAMBURI NATURE TRAIL ✪✪✪

Less than 30 years ago, Bamburi Nature Trail was a stark quarry, excavated by the neighbouring Bamburi Cement Factory. Today, it is a triumph of natural reclamation, superbly landscaped and converted into a wildlife sanctuary and farm. From the entrance, a short walk through beautiful forest leads to the main reception area where two giant Aldabra tortoises keep the lawns carefully cropped. Thick forests of casuarina hide the game sanctuary area where there are hippo, buffalo, zebra, waterbuck, oryx, eland and giraffe.

Commercial activities centre on tilapia, a type of fresh-water fish, and crocodile breeding, as well as forest nurseries. Look out for the two huge baobab trees, planted separately in honour of current and past presidents, Daniel Moi and Jomo Kenyatta respectively.

✚ 31A3
🕐 Daily dawn–dusk
💵 Free
❓ Free guided walks. Best time to visit is after the rains
↔ Gedi ruins (➤ 38); Kipepeo Butterfly Farm (➤ 39)

✚ 31A2
✉ PO Box 81995, Malindi Road
☎ 011-485729
🕐 Daily 9–5 (feeding time 4)
🍴 Barbecue restaurant on premises (£)
💵 Moderate
↔ Bombolulu Workshops and Cultural Centre (➤ 37)

Bamburi Nature Trail safari – just a few yards from beach and hotels

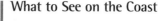

BOMBOLULU WORKSHOPS AND CULTURAL CENTRE

Bombolulu Workshops was founded in 1969 as a rehabilitation centre for physically handicapped local people. Today it employs over 260 people, principally in the manufacture of traditional craft items, and is the largest project of its kind in Kenya. Although it is self-funding, it has gained international sponsorship and its top-quality hand-printed fashion fabrics feature in several well-known charity catalogues. An excellent cultural centre and restaurant has recently been added, making this the most informative and, for many visitors, the most heartening excursion on the Kenyan coast.

A tour of Bombolulu begins with a look at six traditional homesteads, showing how a cross-section of different coastal tribes live, work, eat, sleep and play. The most fascinating of these represents the Mijikende tribe, where a witch doctor demonstrates various beliefs, worships and practices (even today the Mijikende are renowned as sorcerers in Kenya). Meanwhile, throughout the day, musicians, drummers and dancers perform while visitors take lunch or just light refreshments. The tour continues through a series of workshops and finishes in the extensive factory shop (► 107). The workshops are signposted just off the main road, behind the sprawling roadside shantytown of Bombolulu, a compelling and colourful place of ramshackle shelters and vibrant streetlife, which provides a striking and poignant contrast to the five-star hotel resorts a few metres along the coast.

DIANI BEACH (► 18, TOP TEN)

+ 31A2
✉ PO Box 83988 Mombasa
☎ 011-471704, 011-473571
🕐 Showrooms: Mon–Sat 8–6; workshops: Mon–Fri 8–12:45, 2–5; Cultural Centre Mon–Sat 8–5
🍴 Ziga Restaurant (► 92)
Cultural Centre/ workshops – moderate; showroom – free
↔ Bamburi Quarry Nature Trail (► 36)

Handle with care: rock python at Bamburi

➕ 31A3
☎ 0122-32065
🕐 Daily 7–6
✋ Gedi: cheap; Giriama
Village: no set entrance
fee, your Gedi guide will
advise you on a
contribution (cheap)
↔ Watamu (➤ 26), Arabuko
Sokoke Forest (➤ 36),
Kipepeo Butterfly Farm
(➤ 39)

*The atmospheric ruins
of Gedi are reputedly
haunted and shunned
by the locals*

GEDI RUINS ✪✪

Swallowed by the forest and shrouded in mystery, the
Gedi ruins are the romantic remains of a Swahili town
which flourished between the 13th and early 17th
centuries. Archaeological finds indicate that this was once
a trading port with the East (the sea has long since
retreated), and it was destroyed on two occasions, by
Mombasa around 1530, and again in the 18th century by
the vandalistic Galla tribe. Little else is known about Gedi,
however, and given its many fine buildings it is curiously
absent from any historical records.

Only a fraction of Gedi has been excavated, but this
does include the Great Mosque and Palace, built in the
15th and 16th centuries, with several original features still
quite apparent. An impressive pillar tomb stands near by.
Most of the other houses are now only knee high and are
named after their finds, such as House of the Scissors and
House of the Ivory Box. Around 2,500 people once dwelt
here, though only the rich would have lived in the stone
town, with the majority in mud-and-thatch huts.

The Giriama village was established originally as a
tourist attraction, comprising around six different buildings,
but is now lived in permanently by a large extended
Giriama tribe family. The village is of some interest, though
the display of dancing is so lacklustre as to be embar-
rassing.

JUMBA LA MTWANA ✪

The name of this small ruined Swahili town translates as
House of Slaves, though like Gedi (above), which it
resembles in miniature, there is little evidence of what
really went on here. It was deserted in the 16th century,
possibly as the result of tribal warfare. Follow the path
down to the sea where the Mosque by the Sea is the best
preserved of three mosques. There is a pleasant small
beach here, too.

➕ 31A2
✉ PO Box 82412
☎ 011-485543
🕐 Daily dawn–dusk
✋ Cheap

KENYA MARINELAND

Claiming to be the largest snake park and aquarium on the coast, Kenya Marineland is located on Mtwapa Creek and is marketed as a dhow day-trip package, with pick-ups from all the major Mombasa coast hotels. The natural highlight of the trip is the 8km journey along the creek; everything else – Masai dancing, fire eaters, limbo dancers, acrobats – is extremely contrived, though good fun if you're in the mood. Snakes can be handled in the snake park, you can see crocodiles and fish feeding, and also sharks and stingrays taken from the Indian Ocean.

31A2
011-485248
Daily 8:30–6
Expensive

KIPEPEO BUTTERFLY FARM

The Kipepeo Project ('butterfly' in Swahili) is an admirable enterprise set up to sell local butterfly pupae to European and American butterfly attractions. It raises revenue and provides employment for local people; in 1996 over 150 households participated in collecting 18,000 pupae, earning over $21,000, a sizeable amount in such a poor area. At the same time it helps to conserve the Arabuko Sokoke Forest (➤ 36) by showing that there is an alternative to felling the forest for agriculture. The only disappointment is that its own 'butterfly house' is primitive and small. The best time to visit is after the rains (May to July), when the *kipepeo* are most abundant.

31A3
PO Box 57, Kilifi
0125-22078, 0122-32380
Daily 8–5
Cheap
Arabuko Sokoke Forest
(➤ 36), Gedi ruins
(➤ 38)

Back to basics; the everyday chore of crushing grain demonstrated at Kenya Marineland

What to See in and Around Lamu Town

LAMU FORT ✪

29D2
PO Box 48 Lamu
0121-33073
Daily 7:30–6
Cheap

The Sultan of Oman built this sturdy castle between 1810 and 1820 and it remains the only significant monument in Lamu. Until quite recently it was the island prison; now most of it is occupied by municipal offices, though part is given over to an amateurish natural history exhibition. The latter was intended as a temporary forerunner to an ambitious museum, aquarium, café and restaurant complex. Unfortunately, it has all been put on hold for several years. The best reason for visiting the fort is to enjoy the views from its battlements and to look down on to the busy market.

LAMU MUSEUM ✪✪

29D2
PO Box 48 Lamu
0121-33073
Daily 8–6
Cheap

This is the best place to start a tour of Lamu, to get a potted history of the town, the island, the archipelago and the Swahili culture. There is a reconstruction of a Swahili house, old photographs, traditional costumes and model dhows, but the prize exhibits are the two *siwas* – huge ceremonial fanfare horns made of ivory and brass. These date from around the mid-17th century and are possibly the oldest musical instruments in East Africa. The building is the former British District Commissioner's House, and the cannons outside last saw action in 1892.

Rush hour in Lamu town

MANDA ISLAND ✪✪✪

The beaches on Manda Island are almost as wonderful as Shela Beach (▶ below) and have the advantage of shade, though you will need to take your own refreshments. Most dhow captains will be pleased to take you to Manda and combine the trip with some excellent snorkelling around the reef.

🚩 29D2
🍴 Restaurant and bar at Manda Island Village Resort (£)

MATANDONI ✪

To the west of Lamu Island, the boatyards of Matandoni are one of the the last places in Kenya where dhows are still built by traditional methods. However, dhow-building is not always in progress so enquire before you make the journey.

🚩 29D2
❓ From Lamu town it's around 2 hours by dhow, donkey or on foot; or 30 minutes by speedboat

SHELA BEACH ✪✪✪

The small village of Shela is a pleasant 45-minute walk along the front from Lamu town. Beyond Peponi's hotel (▶ 94, 100) lies a fabulous golden beach that stretches for 12 deserted kilometres. It's jokingly said that there if there are 10 people in sight of each other on Shela Beach then the beach is crowded, but most of the time (Sundays apart) it really is like that. At the village end of the beach are enormous dunes rising to a height of 20m.

Behind Peponi's is the landmark rocket-shaped Friday Mosque, built in 1829. If there is a friendly custodian on duty you may be allowed to walk up the tower and enjoy views over Shela.

Beware!

Tourists have been attacked on the walk between Shela and Lamu town, so beware of carrying anything of value or walking alone. Unpleasant incidents have also occured on the more deserted stretches of Shela Beach, so stay within shouting distance of other people. Beware, too, of the fierce sun – there is no shade here.

🚩 29D2
ℹ️ 5-minute dhow journey from Lamu town jetty

SWAHILI HOUSE MUSEUM ✪

This is a fine example of a small 18th-century Swahili house. Characteristic features include ornate plaster decoration, carved plaster niches (to hold a porcelain collection), and ceilings supported by mangrove poles. If you have already seen these features in the reconstructed house in the Lamu Museum, then the Swahili House doesn't justify the entrance fee.

🚩 29D2
🕐 Daily 8–6
💷 Cheap

Above: *cargo handling at the jetty*

➕ 31A3
✉ Malindi Marine Park, PO
Box 109
☎ 0123-20845
🕐 Daily dawn–dusk
💰 Moderate

*Vasco da Gama was here;
the monument at Malindi
commemorates the
coming of the Europeans*

MALINDI

Malindi has been welcoming European visitors for 500 years, ever since Vasco da Gama dropped anchor here in 1498. An alliance was struck between the powerful city state of Malindi and the Portuguese, and for the next century or so this became the base of operations for Portuguese trading and expansionism. A cross of Lisbon stone was erected at the entrance to the bay where Vasco da Gama landed, and it still stands today.

Today Malindi is, with Diani Beach, the coast's primary package resort. The focus of activities is the beach. The huge main beach stretches northwards to deserted dunes where its waters are muddied by the River Sabaki. The more attractive part is nearer the town, though the beach hawkers here are wearisome. Silversands Beach, south of the Vasco da Gama Cross, is a better bet, and is where many of the hotel resorts are based.

A little further south, at the pleasant beach of Casuarina Point, is the resort's biggest attraction, the Malindi Marine Park. This offers excellent snorkelling on the reef, which, with neighbouring Watamu Marine Park, is home to over 140 species of coral. Malindi is also a deep-sea fishing centre (► 69).

The old town is worth a brief look for local colour and bustle, particularly the fruit market. The largest of its 12 mosques, the modern Juma'a Mosque (by the seafront, opposite the Crafts Market), marks the site of the old slave market. Beside the mosque is a 15th-century pillar tomb.

A Drive from Malindi to Bombolulu

This easy, one-day drive along the well surfaced palm-lined coast road passes ancient Swahili sites and traditional villages to visit the coast's best cultural and shopping centre.

Leave Malindi, south on the B8 (main coast road). After 16km look for the sign (left) to Gedi ruins (► 38), via a dusty track. After visiting the ruins, take the track straight on, through Gedi village, turn right on to the E899 main road (left leads to Watamu) and after 100m turn left back on to the B8. After another 3km, look for the sign to the Arabuko Sokoke Forest (► 36). Continue for 43km to Kilifi Bridge. Immediately across the bridge, turn right to the Mnarani ruins, set on the banks of Kilifi Creek.

Like Gedi, Mnarani is a ruined 17th-century Swahili settlement (only an enthusiast would want to see them both in the same day), but it also enjoys a superb waterside position.

Continue for another 42km to Bamburi, where the Cement Works and neighbouring Nature Trail (► 36) are landmarks. After another 5km is the village of Bombolulu. Drive very slowly and look amid the jumble for the Bombolulu Workshops sign and turning on the right (► 37).

Take lunch here at the Ziga Restaurant.

After lunch drive back on the B8 for 35km. At Kibaoni, turn right and a 5km-long track leads to Takaungu (if you miss this turn simply take the next turn, after about 8km).

This charming village, once a slave port, is strung out along a twisting turquoise creek, overhung by wooded cliffs. At the far end of the village a path leads to a beautiful small beach where you can swim and sunbathe before returning the 71km to Malindi.

A girl from the coastal Giriama tribe, near Malindi

Distance
230km

Time
Allow a full day

Start/end point
Malindi
✚ 31A3

Lunch
Ziga Restaurant (£–££; ► 92)
✉ Bombolulu Cultural Centre
☎ 011-471704

43

➕ 31A2
✉ Links road, Nyali
☎ 011-472709
🕐 Daily 8:30–6:30
🍴 Restaurant on premises
(£–££)
💷 Mamba Village: moderate;
Botanical Garden and
aquarium: cheap
❓ Feeding time daily 5pm

MAMBA CROCODILE VILLAGE ✪

Mamba in Swahili means crocodile, and with over 10,000 in residence this claims to be the largest crocodile farm in Africa. You don't get to see them all as many are kept in hothouse breeding conditions, but the pools that are on public view are pleasantly landscaped, dug from a coral quarry, and make an impressive if nightmarish sight, heaving with hundreds of these antediluvian monsters. The largest, 'Big Daddy', weighs in at around 400kg.

Also on site is a small botanical garden which includes a fine orchid collection and a spiders' corner, and a few fish tanks which masquerade as an 'aquarium'.

➕ 46C1
☎ 011-312744
🕐 Moderate
↔ Mamba Village (see above)

MOMBASA MARINE PARK ✪

This is the newest of the Kenya marine parks, designated in 1986, but sadly much of the reef has already been looted or damaged. None the less, it still offers wonderful opportunities for diving and snorkelling amid a fantastic array of multicoloured fish, and is convenient for the Nyali hotels.

➕ 31A1
↔ Wasini Island and Kisite Marine Park (➤ 25)

SHIMONI ✪✪

Shimoni is the staging post for dhow and snorkelling trips to Wasini Island and Kisite Marine Park (➤ 25). The drive to the little village, 15km along a red *murram* (dirt) road, is very tropical, lined with tall palms. Behind here are coconut, sugar and cashew plantations. In Swahili, *Shimoni* means 'place of the hole', so-named after a huge coral cave whose tunnels stretches for some 20km underground. The entrance is quite close to the jetty and it is thought that slaves were kept here before being shipped north. It is possible to explore the cave (ask locally for a guide) where there are impressive stalactites and tree lianas (creepers). You can still see the slaves' shackles bolted on to the walls.

> ### Did you know ?
>
> *The term Swahili derives from the Arab word* sahel, *meaning coast, and was first used some 1,300 years ago when Arab and Persian traders settled on the East African coast. The Swahili are not a single tribe, but a group of different tribes, connected by a common language.*

TIWI BEACH ❀❀❀

Tiwi Beach is the northern extension of Diani Beach (► 18), and begins at the Mwachema River. Next to the river is the barrel-vaulted Kongo Mosque (also known as the Mwana Mosque and the Diani Persian Mosque), built in the 15th century and the most ancient mosque on the coast. Half-hidden behind the palms and huge baobab trees, from afar it looks extremely atmospheric; close up, however, it's in a poor state of repair.

Unlike Diani Beach, Tiwi is budget-traveller territory. The standard of facilities is therefore not as good as further up the coast, but you not only save money here, there is much less hassle from the beach hustlers. Tiwi Beach accommodation is also very popular with Anglo-Kenyans, and at holiday times it's often fully booked.

WASINI ISLAND (► 25, TOP TEN)

WATAMU (► 26, TOP TEN)

✚ 31A1
🕐 Mosque opening times vary
💰 Cheap
❓ Beware, there have been several robberies in the vicinity of the mosque

Left: *inmates at Mamba Crocodile Village*
Below: *the pleasures of a dhow cruise*

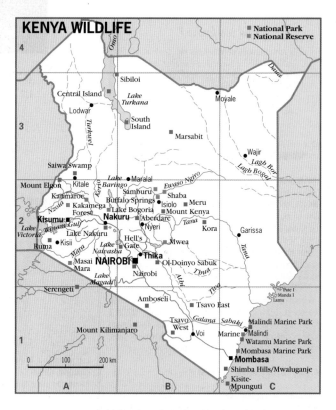

KENYA WILDLIFE

■ National Park
■ National Reserve

Omo
Sibiloi
Central Island   Lake Turkana
Lodwar   Moyale
South Island
Marsabit
Turkwel
Wajir
Lagh Bor
Lagh Bogal
Saiwa Swamp
Kitale   Maralal
Mount Elgon   Lake Baringo   Ewaso Ngiro
Kaimaroe   Samburu   Shaba
Nzoia   Buffalo Springs   Isiolo   Meru
Kakamega   Lake Bogoria   Mount Kenya
Kisumu   Forest   Nakuru   Aberdare   Tana
Lake   Winam Gulf   Lake Nakuru   Nyeri   Kora   Garissa
Victoria   Hell's
Ruma   Kisii   Lake   Gate   Mwea   Tana
Naivasha
Masai   NAIROBI   Thika   Ol-Doinyo Sabuk
Mara   Nairobi   Thua
Lake   Athi
Magadi
Serengeti   Tiwa   Pate I
Amboseli   Manda I
Tsavo East   Lamu
Tsavo   Galana   Sabaki   Malindi Marine Park
Mount Kilimanjaro   West   Voi   Marine   Malindi
Watamu Marine Park
Mombasa Marine Park
0   100   200 km   Mombasa
Shimba Hills/Mwaluganje
Kisite-
Mpunguti

A   B   C

4 · 3 · 2 · 1

What to See in the Southern Game Parks

AMBOSELI NATIONAL PARK (▶ 17, TOP TEN)

MWALUGANJE ELEPHANT SANCTUARY   ✪✪
For a guaranteed sight of elephants in the wild without having to leave the coast, take a Land Rover excursion to the 24,000-hectare Mwaluganje Elephant Sanctuary. This is one of Kenya's more recent conservation projects, established in 1993, and is unique in that local tribes (the Duruma and Digo) are now involved in its day-to-day management and maintenance. Tha sanctuary is easily accessible from Diani Beach or Shimba Lodge.

SHIMBA HILLS NATIONAL RESERVE   ✪✪✪
Shimba Hills is the only game park in the coastal region, yet given its proximity to the popular resort of Diani Beach (a mere 45-minute drive away), it is under-visited. The reserve is an area of

✚ 46C1
☎ 0127-2142, John Clarke for tours
🕐 Daily dawn–dusk
💷 Expensive
↔ Shimba Hills National Reserve (see below)

✚ 46C1
✉ PO Box 30, Kwale
☎ 0127-4159
💷 Very expensive

outstanding unspoiled beauty, its pristine green rolling hills and rich rain forest forming one of Kenya's most picturesque backdrops for game viewing. Many of its giant trees are thought to be over 1,000 years old. Rising to an altitude of up to 450m, the hills offer marvellous views right over to the Indian Ocean, and provide a welcome respite from the humid heat of the coast.

The reserve is home to lions, leopards, buffaloes, elephants, zebras and a small family of giraffes. You should be fortunate to see big cats by day, but the 'quarry' that most visitors seek here is the sable antelope. This is the only sanctuary in Kenya where this magnificent large animal can be seen; the females are chestnut, the males are almost black, and both sport superb sickle-shaped horns. They are mainly active in the early morning and late afternoon. Patience is needed as the undergrowth is so dense it is sometimes difficult to spot the animals.

If you are staying overnight at the Shimba Hills Lodge there is every chance that you will see elephants and buffaloes come to the floodlit waterhole. Leopards are baited (hunks of meat are set out to attract them) and put in the occasional appearance. Visitors may also take guided walks.

🔁 Mwaluganje Elephant Sanctuary
❓ Contact Dick Knight for Shimba Hills tours (☎ 0127-2142)

TAITA HILLS GAME SANCTUARY ✪✪✪

Taita Hills Game Sanctuary lies between Tsavo East and Tsavo West parks (▶ 48–9) and covers 110,000 hectares. The Hills, dramatic mounds rising from the plains, climb to over 2,000m, making this area not only very scenic but better watered than the adjacent savannah of dusty Tsavo. Game viewing is excellent. If you want to watch the animals overnight, stay at Salt Lick Lodge (▶ 105). Waterholes and salt licks have been created and bait is laid out for the nocturnal predators. From here, or from its sister establishment, Taita Hills Lodge, you can also take night drives, guided walks or go ballooning.

🔳 29C1
☎ 02-334000 (Hilton International)
🕐 Daily dawn–dusk
💰 Expensive

Look out for elusive leopards at Shimba Hills

TSAVO EAST NATIONAL PARK   ✪✪✪

Tsavo National Park is split into two parks, Tsavo East and Tsavo West.

Tsavo East is a huge area of monotonous flat semi-arid plains, savannah and scrubland, covering over 11,700sq km. Well over half the park, north of the Galana and the Athi rivers, is closed to the general public (only private safaris may enter), the result of the devastation wrought in the 1970s and 1980s by poachers. It is estimated that in the 1950s there were around 50,000 elephants and between 6,000 and 9,000 rhinos in Tsavo; by the time of the ivory ban in 1989 the elephant herds had been decimated to less than 5,000 and the rhinos had been almost gunned out of existence (only 50–100 survived).

Today, the elephants have recovered and now number around 8,000, forming some of the largest herds in the country. In the dry season, visitors are often amused to see the elephants glowing red after dust baths in the particularly vivid Tsavo soil. Sadly, the chances of seeing rhino are very slim.

The most popular access to Tsavo East is the Voi Gate, with Voi Safari Lodge just inside the park (➤ 105). Close by, the man-made Aruba Dam also has a high concentration of wildlife. Another popular site is Mudanda Rock, which is a magnet for wildlife in the dry season.

✚ 29C2
✉ PO Box 14, Voi
☎ 147-2211, 147-2105
⬚ Very expensive

TSAVO WEST NATIONAL PARK   ✪✪✪

Topographically and scenically, Tsavo West is superior to Tsavo East, with diverse habitats including the Chyulu Hills volcanic mountain range, river forests, wooded grasslands and bubbling springs, as well as great plains. There are sometimes also marvellous views across to Kilimanjaro. Game viewing, however, is more difficult. You will need to visit the specially protected Ngulia Rhino Sanctuary enclosure to view the park's most precious species.

Close by, Ngulia Lodge, next to a watering hole, provides good sedentary game viewing and baits leopard. It is also an ornithological paradise during the short rains each year. Hundreds of thousands of migrating birds pass right overhead and, perhaps disoriented by the lodge floodlights (the reason for its attraction to the birds isn't exactly clear), many stop here.

The star attraction of Tsavo West is Mzima Springs, a pristine pool gushing 250 million litres of water per day, a fraction of which is tapped and piped to form Mombasa'a principal drinking supply. Here, visitors are guaranteed large numbers of crocodiles and hippos. Underwater hides were also constructed for hippo viewing, though unfortunately the hippos rarely now oblige with their presence. Close by, in the northwestern corner of the park, is the spectacular Shetani lava flow.

✚ 29C1
✉ PO Box 14, Voi
☎ 147-2211, 147-2105
🖐 Very expensive

A meeting of the local water buffalo club, Mzima Springs, Tsavo West

Big Game

On safari everyone wants to see the 'Big Five' – lion, leopard, elephant, rhino and buffalo. To see lions visit the Masai Mara, for elephants go to Amboseli or Tsavo. Leopards are the most shy and elusive of all the big game, so try Nakuru or Samburu.

Above: *the king of the beasts,* panthera leo, *at the Masai Mara*

Big Cats

The lion is the biggest of all Africa's cats. The average male (distinguished by its mane) weighs around 200kg. Lions usually live in prides of 10 to 20 animals. The leopard is long, low and powerfully built, with clustered rings of dark spots. It is a solitary creature and if you see one it will probably be in the branches of a tree. Sleek and elegant, the cheetah is also spotted, but is much smaller than the leopard and lives in small groups. It is the world's fastest land animal, capable of speeds of around 100kph over a short distance.

Antelope and Zebra

The most common antelope are Thomson's gazelle, Grant's gazelle and impala. All are tawny in colour, with horns. The impala is the largest of the three; the males have elegant lyre-shaped horns.

The biggest of all the antelopes (1.7m–2m at the shoulder) is the eland, with a cow-like body and spiral horns. Two other notable, handsome heavyweights are the beisa oryx, found in the north, and the sable antelope, found only in the Shimba Hills. Both have black-and-white striped faces and large horns. The commonly seen waterbuck is easily distinguished by its dark, grey-brown

Above: *the ubiquitous impala*
Right: *Grevy's zebra (found in the north)*

shaggy coat. The wildebeest (or gnu) which stars in the great annual migration spectacle (► 116), is a strange looking animal with features of both ox and horse. Zebra are wild horses. Burchell's zebra is the ubiquitous variety, while the rare Grevy's zebra, found in the Samburu region, features narrow, symmetrical stripes.

The High and Mighty

The African elephant is the biggest land animal on earth. The average adult weighs over 5.5 tonnes. The elephant is intelligent and exhibits sophisticated social behaviour. The rare black rhino is the only rhino indigenous to Kenya. The white rhino, imported from South Africa, is actually the same grey colour as the black rhino. The buffalo (or Cape buffalo) is a huge ox-like creature with heavy horns, and is just as dangerous, when aroused, as its fellow heavyweights. The hippo measures up to 1.7m high at the shoulder and spends most of its day in water, coming out to graze at night. It is claimed to be responsible for more deaths in Africa than any other animal – generally as a result of turning over boats.

Kenya also features the world's tallest animal, the giraffe, measuring up to 6m. The common giraffe in southern Kenya is the Masai; Rothschild giraffe is found in Nakuru (► 77) and the reticulated giraffe is a native of the Samburu region.

Top: *rhino at Nyeri*
Above: *reticulated giraffe*
Below: *the mighty elephant*

Nairobi

Nairobi, the largest city in East Africa, is a dusty place of broken pavements, peeling colonial buildings and state-of-the-art skyscrapers. Visitors' Nairobi, if such a thing exists, is the small central area bounded by Moi, Harambee and Uhuru avenues and stretching north past the Norfolk Hotel to the National Museum. Within this area, *wazungu* (whites) are always hustled but usually safe.

The city centre has few tourist sights and none are essential viewing, but to omit it is to miss out an important part of the real Kenya.

At least one day should also be spent enjoying the various suburban attractions and the Nairobi National Park.

'Nairobi is like a balloon
floating high aloft,
but stationary, where
Europeans are
overworked and
important, and the rest
of East Africa a
distant blur.'

ELSPETH HUXLEY
The Sorcerer's Apprentice
(1948)

The Hilton Hotel

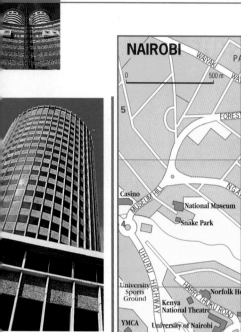

NAIROBI

PARKLANDS

WAIYAKI WAY

0   500 m

5

FOREST ROAD

FOREST ROAD

LUMURU ROAD

UMURU ROAD

NGARA ROAD

Casino

MUSEUM HILL

National Museum

Snake Park

4

University Sports Ground

UHURU HIGHWAY

HARRY THUKU ROAD

Norfolk Hotel

Kenya National Theatre

Central Police Station

Nairobi

KIRINYAGA

YMCA

University of Nairobi

UNIVERSITY WAY

MOI AVENUE

MANGA ROAD

Ismaili Khoja Mosque

Post Office

TOM MBOYA

3

Synagogue

Jevanjee Gardens

St Paul's Chapel

KOINANGE

French Cultural Centre

MUINDI MBINGU

BIASHARA STREET

McMillan Library

KIMATHI STREET

St Andrew's Church

Goethe Institute

Jamia Mosque

British Council

MOI AVENUE

City Market

WABERA

Gallery Watatu

African Heritage Centre

War Mem

UHURU

Galton Fenzi Mem

KENYATTA AVE

MAMA NGINA STREET

Central Park

Nairobi Province HQ (Nyayo House)

Post Office

KAUNDA ST

City Hall

Law Courts

TAIFA RD

2

Holy Family Cathedral

CITY SQUARE

CITY HALL WAY

Inter-Continental Hotel

HIGHWAY

KENYATTA AVENUE

Uhuru Park

PARLIAMENT ROAD

Kenyatta International Conference Centre

Sheria House

Jogoo House

All Saints Cathedral

Jomo Kenyatta Mausoleum

HARAMBEE AVE

NGONG ROAD

Parliament Building

Donovan Maule Theatre

HAILE SELASSIE

1

Railway Sports Ground

NGONG ROAD

HAILE SELASSIE AVENUE

Railway Museum

UHURU HIGHWAY

Golf Course

A

B

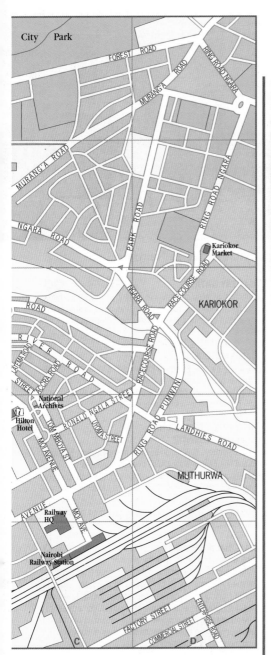

The Uhuru (Freedom)
Monument at Langata

Eastern delight; Jamia Mosque

54B2

Standard Street, PO Box 41855

02-228737

Mon–Sat 9–6, Sun 10–5

Free

54B3

54B2

City Square, PO Box 30746

02-332383

Mon–Fri 9:30–12:30, 2–4:30

Free

55C2

Moi Avenue, PO Box 49210

02-228959

Mon–Fri 8:30–4:30, Sat 8–1

Free

What to See in Nairobi

GALLERY WATATU
This highly rated commercial gallery shows off some of the best of Kenya's contemporary works, as well as sculptures and paintings by over 30 artists from all over East Africa.

JAMIA MOSQUE
In a city centre of very dubious architectural taste, the ornate green-and-white Jamia Mosque is a delight. Unfortunately non-Muslims are not welcome here so you will have to admire it from outside.

KENYATTA INTERNATIONAL CONFERENCE CENTRE
This 28-storey, 105m-high building is the tallest in Kenya. It is the headquarters for KANU (the ruling political party) and boasts a huge conference auditorium. On a clear day you can see all the way from Kilimanjaro to Mount Kenya from its roof-top walkway, but even on a dull day the swarming hordes below and the countryside stretching beyond is a fascinating contrast.

NATIONAL ARCHIVES
The entrance hall of this handsome classical building (1906) contains one of the country's more bizarre sights, heaped haphazardly in the centre of the floor. Objects range from oriental carpets and Indian chests to African masks, drums and other ethnographic artefacts. Unfortunately there's virtually no information on the exhibits, you can't get close to them (they're cordoned off) and the room is extremely dimly lit.

NATIONAL MUSEUM OF KENYA ✪

This wide-ranging collection is a reasonable introduction to the country's natural history, and to its human prehistoric importance. Most of the displays, however, are resolutely old-fashioned and in dire need of repair.

The Prehistory Hall exhibits skulls and skeletons which have helped shape the universal theory of prehistory, and details the pioneering works of the Leakeys.

Displayed around the main staircase are the beautiful portraits by Joy Adamson (➤ 14) of the different tribes of Kenya, while downstairs are her works of art depicting Kenya's flora. On the upper floor are various ethnographic artefacts. Adjacent is the colourful Gallery of Contemporary East African Art.

🕀 54A4
✉ Museum Road
☎ 02-742161
🕐 Daily 9:30–6
🍴 Café Bustani on premises (£)
✋ Cheap

> ### *Did you know ?*
>
> *In 1898, work was severely disrupted on the Uganda Railway line when two lions devoured 30 or so of the Indian workmen building the line through Tsavo. The lions were eventually shot by Lt Colonel J H Patterson, who later recounted the epic story in his book* The Man-Eaters of Tsavo. *The 1997 Michael Douglas film,* The Ghost and the Darkness, *brought it to the big screen.*

RAILWAY MUSEUM ✪

The Railway Museum is dedicated to the historic East Africa/Uganda Railway, originally derided as 'The Lunatic Line', because no one knew where it was going, who would use it or what it would cost (➤ 10). Note the railway car in which Charles Ryall placed himself in 1899 as bait to tempt a man-eating Tsavo lion. Tragically he fell asleep while waiting, was dragged from the car by the lion and devoured.

🕀 54B1
✉ Off Haile Selassie Avenue
☎ 02-221211
🕐 Daily 8:30–4:45 (closes 3:30 Sat)
✋ Cheap
❓ Beware, there have been robberies along the road between here and the railway station. Approach instead from Haile Selassie Avenue

Nostalgic reminders of the pioneering spirit at the Railway Museum

What to See in Nairobi Environs

Driving in and around Nairobi is not recommended. Either join the organised excursions which run to most of the following sights or hire a taxi for a day (all sights are close to each other). Bus No 24 goes to most of these, but public transport is not recommended.

BOMAS OF KENYA ⊗⊗

The Bomas (traditional homesteads) of Kenya is a cultural and entertainment centre where a number of small villages have been set up to show the architecture, culture and customs of Kenya's principal tribes. Most of the energy of the guides, however, is channelled into selling handicrafts. Every afternoon dancers perform in an auditorium and while it's an energetic and colourful spectacle, it somehow lacks conviction and authenticity – probably because it is a single (professional) troupe who quick change through the various costumes and represent all the different tribes.

✚ 62B2
✉ Forest Edge Road
☎ 02-891801
🕐 Mon–Fri 9–5, Sat & Sun 1–6 (dancing 2:30 weekdays, 3:30 weekends)
♿ Moderate

THE (LANGATA) GIRAFFE CENTRE ⊗⊗⊗

If there's one single site in Kenya that has universal appeal and charm then it's this one. Visitors feed Rothschild giraffes with small pellets on a special observation tower which brings them up to the giraffes' height. This may not sound particularly exciting, but the sensation of hand-feeding such huge, beautiful, gentle creatures is unforgettable and is an unexpected highlight of many a Kenya trip. For children it's a magical experience.

The serious purpose behind this project is to save the Rothschild giraffe from extinction. In 1973, its numbers were down to 130. Today, thanks to the African Fund for Endangered Wildlife (which manages the Giraffe Centre) numbers have reached 500 and are growing.

✚ 62B2
✉ Gogo Falls Road, off Langata South Road, Langata
☎ 02-891658, 02-890952
🕐 Mon–Fri 2–5:30, Sat & Sun 10–5:30, school holidays daily 11–5:30 (closed weekday mornings to allow school visits)
🍴 Café on premises (£)
♿ Moderate

Close encounters

KAREN BLIXEN MUSEUM

No one who has read the book or seen the film *Out of Africa* (►14) will want to miss this little house 'at the foot of the Ngong Hills'. The interior is suitably atmospheric, though there's not a lot to see and the short guided tour is indeed short. Of note is Karen Blixen's beautiful painting of her servant girl Ndito. It's interesting, too, to see the similarity between the young Blixen and Meryl Streep, who played her in the film. Most of the furniture here is contemporary (but not original), left behind by Universal Pictures after the film.

Don't leave without sitting in the garden for a few minutes. It's a beautiful tranquil spot, and gazing over to the Ngong Hills it's easy to imagine yourself back in the Africa of the 1920s.

🛏 62B2
✉ Karen Road
☎ 02-822779
🕐 Daily 9:30–6
🍴 Horseman Restaurant (►92)
💰 Cheap

Karen Blixen's dining room

NAIROBI NATIONAL PARK

The most remarkable thing about this park is that it exists at all, so close to such a major city. To quote one fortunate local resident – 'we had a couple of hours to spare on Sunday, so we popped into the park and saw a leopard, a rhino, and a giraffe giving birth.'

The classic view features herds of zebra or antelope backed by the Nairobi skyscrapers. For some visitors it's a facinating juxtaposition, for others it's an unwelcome intrusion. Whatever your opinion, there is no denying that this is a good introduction to Kenya's wildlife. The park is largely flat, open savannah – rather uninspiring, but good for spotting numbers of antelope, zebra, buffalo and giraffe. The park has the country's largest breeding population of black rhino (63 at the last count), and hippos may be seen at the pretty river walk where groups often stop for a picnic. Lions, cheetahs and leopards are elusive, but the only large absentee is the elephant. Birdlife is prolific, with over 400 species.

🛏 62B2
✉ PO Box 42076
☎ 02-50108
🕐 Daily 6:15–6
🍴 The Carnivore (►92)
💰 Expensive

NGONG HILLS

These beautiful hills, immortalised in *Out of Africa*, stretch up beyond the suburb of Karen (named after Karen Blixen, (►14) and are the perfect place to stretch your legs. On the eastern side there are panoramic views back over to Nairobi and its suburbs, and to the west a short 20- to 30-minute walk (from the ranger post up to the aerial masts on the spine of the hills) offers a dramatic look into the Rift Valley (►23). For the clearest views, come early morning.

Due to security problems you will be accompanied by an armed ranger.

🛏 62B2
💰 Free
🍴 Horseman Restaurant (►92)

The Central Highlands

The Central Highlands mainly comprise the Aberdare Range and Mount Kenya, the second-highest mountain in Africa. Below their lofty peaks lie Kenya's most fertile and productive farmlands, a point not lost on the British settlers who colonised and intensively cultivated this area, giving the term 'the White Highlands' a meaning over and above its snow-capped summits.

These days few of the huge colonial estates remain, carved up at the time of independence and returned to the Kikuyu people, who have always regarded the area as sacred land, given to them by God.

The refined, luxurious atmosphere of the colonial days still lives on, however, at the Aberdare Country Club, the Outspan Hotel, the Mount Kenya Safari Club and a handful of other establishments.

'A more charming region is not to be found in all Africa.'

JOSEPH THOMSON
Through Masailand: To the Central African Lakes and Back
(1883)

Magnificent view from the Aberdare Country Club

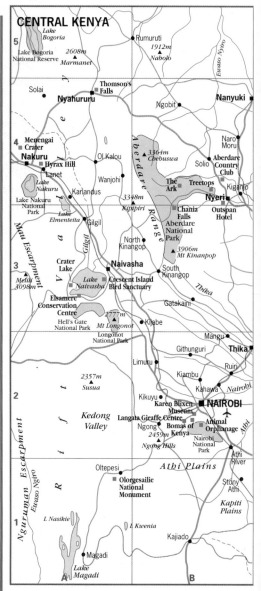

CENTRAL KENYA

Lake Bogoria

Lake Bogoria National Reserve

2608m ▲ Marmanet

Rumuruti ●

1912m ▲ Nabolo

Ewaso Nyiro

Solai ●

Thomson's Falls

Nyahururu ■

Ngobit ●

Nanyuki ■

4 Menengai ▪ Crater

Nakuru ■
■ **Hyrax Hill**
Lanet

Ol Kalou ●

Wanjohi ●

Lake Nakuru

3364m Chebuswa

Aberdare Range

Naro Moru ●

Solio ●

Aberdare Country Club

The Ark ■ Treetops ■

Kiganjo ●

Kariandus

3348m ▲ Kipipiri

Nyeri ■

Chania Falls ■

Outspan Hotel ■

Lake Nakuru National Park

Gilgil

Lake Elmenteita

Gilgil

North Kinangop ●

Naivasha ●

Aberdare National Park

3906m ▲ Mt Kinanpop

3 Crater Lake

Mau Escarpment

Melili ▲ 3098m

Lake Naivasha

Crescent Island Bird Sanctuary

South Kinangop

Thika

Gatakaini ●

Elsamere Conservation Centre

2777m ▲ Mt Longonot

● Kijabe

Hell's Gate National Park

Longonot National Park

Mangu ●

Thika ■

Githunguri ●

Ruiri ●

Limuru ●

2357m ▲ Susua

Kiambu ●

Kahawa *Nairobi*

Kikuyu ●

Karen Blixen Museum

Langata Giraffe Centre

2 Kedong Valley

Ngong ● **Bomas of Kenya**

2459m ▲ Ngong Hills

■ **NAIROBI**

Animal Orphanage ■

Nairobi National Park

Athi

Nguruman Escarpment

Ewaso Ngiro

Rift

Oltepesi ●

■ **Olorgesailie National Monument**

Athi Plains

Athi River ●

Stony Athi ●

Kapiti Plains

1 L Nasikie

L Kwenia

Kajiado ●

Magadi ●

Lake Magadi

A   *B*

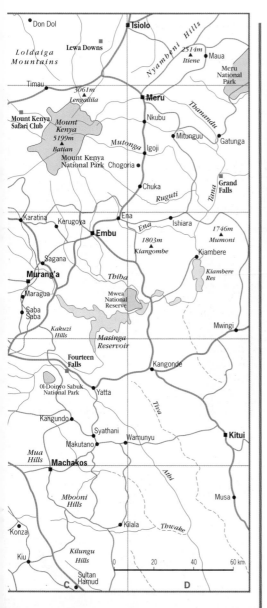

Manicured lawns in the heart of Africa

A Drive Through the Aberdares

Distance
112km

Time
A full day

Start/end point
Nyeri
62B4

Lunch
Pack a picnic

This journey through marvellous landscapes requires a four-wheel-drive vehicle; hiring a driver is recommended. Go only in dry weather as even four-wheel-drive vehicles can get stuck in the wet. Before setting off call the warden (☎ 170-55024) to ask about road conditions.

From Nyeri take the main road (B5) towards Nyahururu for 2km, then turn left on the D435, signposted to Ruhuruini Gate and Aberdare National Park. After almost 8km, having passed the Italian Memorial Church on your right, you come to Ihururu village. Turn right at the village (signed Kimathi School) and follow signs (keep turning right) to the National Park Gate.

The road climbs steadily for another 6km. Once through the Ruhuruini Gate the road winds even more steeply.

Eventually you will climb out on to open moorland, at a height of over 3,000m. Shortly after this (17km from the park gate) fork left. Continue for another 6km and a turning to the left, just past the campsites, leads to the 25m-high Chania Falls.

This is a wonderful spot for a picnic. It is a 10-minute walk down to the bottom and it's best to make plenty of noise in case there is any wildlife en route.

Continue for another 4.7km, then turn left. After 1.8km turn right (a turning shortly on the left leads to a self-help Fishing Camp) and drive on for another 6.5km to a timber platform.

The Chania Falls, where Winston Churchill camped while on safari in 1907

From here there are marvellous views of the giant 275m-high Karuru Falls. The 300m-high Gura Falls (the highest in Kenya) can be seen in the distance.

Retrace your route back to Nyeri.

THE ABERDARE RANGE (► 16, TOP TEN)

THE ARK AND ABERDARE COUNTRY CLUB ✪✪✪

The Ark was designed on biblical lines and from afar resembles the popular conception of Noah's vessel. Inside, it's a comfortable modern lodge with large balconies, picture-window viewing areas and a ground-level bunker hide. Its position, right in the mountain forest, ensures a good mix of game viewing, including elephants, rhinos and occasionally big cats.

A raised walkway from the Ark gives the opportunity for visitors to stretch their legs and look down into the jungle. Before entry to the Ark there is also the option of a game drive around the Aberdare Salient, an area rich in rain forest and where most of the Aberdares' animals are to be found.

Entrance to the Ark is via the Aberdare Country Club, a charming piece of Kenya, offering magnificent views over the top of the Aberdares. Its grounds also include a game sanctuary, a swimming pool and various activities (► 69).

- 62B4
- ✉ Aberdare Country Club and Ark, PO Box 449, Nyeri
- ☎ 0171-55620
- 🕓 Day membership Mon–Thu: cheap; Fri–Sun: moderate (includes use of swimming pool & admission to game sanctuary). The Ark is only open to overnight guests (► 103). Aberdare Salient Game Drive (Ark guests only): very expensive

LEWA DOWNS ✪✪✪

Currently one of Kenya's most fashionable private parks, Lewa Downs is a combination of cattle ranch, game park and black rhino sanctuary. It is most famous for its rhino conservation, but hosts a large range of game including big cats, elephants, eland, hartebeests, greater kudu and northern species such as gerenuks, reticulated giraffes and Grevy's zebras. It also offers horse riding, bush walks and night game-drives. Admittance is only to overnight guests staying at the Wilderness Trails Lodge (► 105).

- 63C5
- ✉ PO Box 14398, Isiolo

MOUNT KENYA (► 22, TOP TEN)

MOUNT KENYA SAFARI CLUB ✪✪✪

Sited in the foothills of Mount Kenya, with magnificent views of the mountain, and literally straddling the Equator, this is one of the world's finest hotels (► 103). Its manicured grounds include a glorious swimming pool and a lake which is home to sacred ibises and marabou storks.

The original estate was built in the 1930s, but it was the Texas oil millionaire Ray Ryan and American film star William Holden who transformed it in 1959 into a meeting place for the rich, the royal and the famous. Temporary membership is accorded to overnight guests and day membership is also possible. It's worth the expense, not only to see how the other half lives, but to take lunch and to visit the Animal Orphanage. You can see several rare animals that are part of a captive breeding programme.

- 63C4
- ✉ PO Box 35, Nanyuki
- ☎ 0176-22960
- 🕓 Temporary day membership: moderate (includes use of swimming pool & bowling green). Animal Orphanage: expensive

A Walk on Mount Kenya

Mount Kenya, seen from the Aberdare Forest

Distance
24km (return)

Time
The total walking time from the Met Station to Mackinder's Camp is 4–6 hours one-way, but you will need a minimum of 1½ days including an overnight stay on the mountain (discuss with your guide)

Start/end point
Naro Moru
⊞ 62B4

Lunch
Arrange food supplies with your guide
(Note: The route/arrangements will vary according to your guide)

Mount Kenya is one of only a small number of great mountains whose summit is accessible to non-climbers. However, unless you are used to climbing at altitude it is best to allow five days for the full ascent.

The following walk is suggested for those who do not have this amount of time but would still like to sample the mountain. Make your guiding and transport arrangements either with Naro Moru River Lodge, at Naro Moru on the A2 (☎ 0176-62212) or the Naro Moru Youth Hostel, located on the Naro Moru route road (just off the A2, opposite the Naro Moru River Lodge – no telephone). Go only during the dry season.

You will be driven from Naro Moru up through the main park gate, through thick tropical bamboo forest, across the Percival Bridge (over a deep ravine), until you reach the Meteorological Station, at an altitude of 3,000m. Here your walk begins.

After walking for about 40 minutes the forest ends abruptly and you come out on to open moorland with superb views (in good weather) across the Aberdares. The next section, which takes about three hours, is known as the Vertical Bog, awful in wet weather, but manageable in the dry season. From hereon, you will see extraordinary moorland plants, such as giant groundsel. As you come out on to the ridge above the Teleki Valley there is a spectacular view of the main peaks.

Continue on to Mackinder's Camp, at 4,200m, where you will spend the night.

The return to the Met Station the next morning takes around two to three hours.

NANYUKI ⭐

One of Kenya's more attractive provincial towns, Nanyuki retains something of its colonial feel with the Settlers' Store, its most famous landmark, built in 1938.

South of the town are two Equator signs where, amid a horde of souvenir sellers, the famous 'Equator water phenomenon' is demonstrated. Armed with a funnel, a supply of water and two matchsticks, the Nanyuki locals show how the water swirls down the funnel clockwise in the northern hemisphere, then by stepping just a few metres across the line into the southern hemisphere, how the direction changes to anti-clockwise.

TREETOPS ⭐⭐

Treetops opened in 1932 as Kenya's original jungle tree-house, a modest two-room affair, supposedly inspired by *Peter Pan*. Twenty years later it still had only four rooms, but gained world-wide fame as the place where Princess Elizabeth learned of the death of her father and therefore of her accession to the throne as Queen of England. The original Treetops burned down soon after and was rebuilt in romantic style with 50 rooms.

Unfortunately for visitors these days, elephant destruction has obliterated so much of the surrounding tree cover that Treetops is no longer in the forest and this deters the presence of smaller animals. None the less it remains hugely popular (▶ 103).

The entrance to Treetops is via the Outspan Hotel (▶ 103) which features several leisure and sporting facilities and from where there are game drives to the Aberdare Salient and walks along the Chania River.

✚ 62B4

✉ Outspan Hotel, PO Box 24

☎ Outspan Hotel 0171-2424. Booking for Outspan and Treetops 02-540780

ℹ Treetops is only open to overnight guests. Day-rate for Outspan Hotel: cheap

✚ 62B4

The Equator Line, Nanyuki

In the Know

If you only have a short time to visit Kenya, or would like to get a real flavour of the country, here are some ideas:

10 Ways To Be A Local

Read the *Daily Nation*.
Hire a bicycle on the coast.
Seek out some authentic Swahili or African dishes. Hotels occasionally serve them; if not ask.
Shop at fixed price co-operatives and self-help groups to help the locals.
Never criticise the government in front of a black Kenyan; he may agree with your point of view but it's a sensitive issue.
Try to get to a local feast or *nyama choma* (➤ 80) or authentic nightspot with Kenyan or African music (you'll need to be accompanied by a local).
Stay in an old Swahili house in Lamu town.

Masai woman

Ballooning over the Masai Mara

Wander around the local towns and market (take a guide).
Ask someone to teach you a few bars of the famous *Jambo Bwana* song. It's easy to sing, terribly infectious and will get broad smiles wherever you go.
Whatever the hassle, stay calm. Try to remember the people hassling you are generally very poor by western standards and know no other way of selling their wares.
(➤ 92–9 for further details)

10 Good Places To Have Lunch

Crater Lake Camp, Lake Naivasha (➤ 99).
Hemingway's, Watamu (➤ 95).
The Horseman, Karen (➤ 98).
Mount Kenya Safari Club, near Nanyuki (➤ 103).
Nomad's, Diani Beach (➤ 93).
The Norfolk Hotel, Delamere Terrace, Nairobi (➤ 96).
Peponi Hotel, Shela, Lamu Island (➤ 100).
Thomson Falls Lodge, near Nyahururu (➤ 99).
The Thorn Tree Café, New Stanley Hotel, Nairobi (➤ 97).
Wasini Island Restaurant (➤ 95).

10
Top Activities

Ballooning: Mara Balloon Safaris, Governor's Camp, Masai Mara; Taita Hills (➤ 47).
Big Game fishing (August to May): Hemingways, Watamu; Ocean Sports, Watamu; John Clark, Diani Beach; Driftwood Club, Malindi.
Diving (September to April): many coastal hotels offer facilities. Specialists include: Aqua Ventures at Ocean Sports, Watamu; Driftwood Club, Malindi; Kisite Marine Park Dhow Tours (➤ 25); Peponi's, Shela Beach, Lamu.
Golf: Nyali Golf & Country Club; Diani Golf Club; Mount Kenya Safari Club (➤ 65); Aberdare Country Club (➤ 62–3).
Horse riding: in Masailand, near the Masai Mara park, with Safaris Unlimited; Mount Kenya Safari Club (➤ 65); Aberdare Country Club (➤ 62–3).
Horse-racing: Nairobi race course, 10km southwest of city centre. Open most Sundays (except August and September). Look in *The Sunday Nation*.
Snorkelling (September to April): Kisite Marine Park (➤ 25); Watamu Marine Park (➤ 26); Lamu/Manda (➤ 40–1); Malindi (➤ 42).
Walking: Galana River (Tsavo East) with Tropical Ice; Chyulu Hills (Tsavo West) and Loita Hills (southern Rift Valley) with

Safari on horseback means you can get much closer to grazing animals

Savage Wilderness Safaris.
White-water rafting: on the Athi River with Savage Wilderness Safaris.
Windsurfing: at Diani Beach several hotels offer board hire and tuition. Peponi's, Shela Beach, Lamu.

5
Memorable Views

- Rift Valley from just below Iten (➤ 23).
- Masai Mara from a balloon (➤ 20–1 and Top Activities, above).
- Tsavo East from Voi Safari Lodge (➤ 48).
- Kilimanjaro from Amboseli National Park (➤ 17).
- Western Kenya from Mount Elgon (➤ 89).

5
Vital Tips For Drivers

- Carry plenty of water, and an emergency needle kit in case you have an accident and need an injection.
- Learn how to change a wheel for *when* (not if) you get a puncture. Check you have all the necessary tools when hiring the car.
- If you see the President's car (flanked by motorbike outriders with flashing lights) you *must* get off the road and stop immediately.
- Don't drive at night.
- Keep your doors locked and windows up when travelling through urban areas. Air-conditioning is vital for comfort if you're travelling any distance. (➤ 117–23)

69

The Rift Valley

The Rift Valley shears through Kenya from Lake Turkana in the north to Lake Magadi in the south, crossing from inhospitable desert through fertile farming country and back to desert. It is a fascinating volcanic landscape, and although most activity ceased some 2 million years ago, forces are still at work.

For the majority of visitors the Rift Valley means Kenya's Lake District, and most safaris out of Nairobi include Lake Baringo and Lake Nakuru, while increasingly Lake Bogoria and Lake Naivasha feature on the schedules. Visitors don't come here for big game – most animals have long been dispersed by human settlement, but ornithologists come for the fascinating birdlife.

'Naivasha is a paradise. The delicate browns of the grass, the ever-changing lake and the airy blue-bleu horizon – it is like a beautiful delicate old painting.'

KAREN BLIXEN
on Lake Naivasha (the 'Pearl of the Rift Valley'),
Letters From Africa

Fischer's Tower at Hell's Gate Park is a reminder of the area's volcanic history

+ 62A3
⊙ Dawn–dusk
✋ Cheap

+ 62A3
⊠ Moi South Lake Road, PO Box 1497, Naivasha
☎ 311-21055
⊙ Daily 3–6PM
¶ Lunch (al fresco buffet) by appointment (£)
✋ Cheap

+ 62A3
⊠ PO Box 234, South Lake Road, Naivasha
☎ 311-20510
⊙ Daily dawn–dusk
✋ Expensive
↔ Lake Naivasha (➤ 75)

CRATER LAKE ✪✪✪
This brilliant jade green lake has been formed in the crater of an extinct volcano right on the edge of Lake Naivasha (➤ 75, 76). Until very recently it was unknown – a secret world. Now it is officially protected as a game sanctuary, home to colobus monkeys and plains game. For human creature comforts there is a luxury tented camp (➤ 104).

ELSAMERE CONSERVATION CENTRE ✪✪
Set on the beautiful banks of Lake Naivasha (➤ 75, 76) this was the home of Joy Adamson (➤ 14) from 1968 until 1980. Today it functions as a conservation centre and a small museum. Visitors can watch *The Joy Adamson Story* video, look round the museum and take afternoon tea (served at 4PM) on the lovely lawns where colobus monkeys are frequent visitors. The centre also provides accommodation (➤ 104).

HELL'S GATE NATIONAL PARK ✪✪✪
The principal feature of Hell's Gate National Park is the Njorowa Gorge. This is an old outlet of Lake Naivasha, long since dried up and now famous for its huge eroded cliffs which reach a height of 150m. At the entrance to the gorge stands Fischer's Tower, a much-photographed 25m-tall needle of red rock, once a volcanic plug.

There are two other notable extinct volcanoes in the park – Olkaria and Hobley's. You will also see natural steam vents rising from fissures in the rock, and at the western end of the gorge this energy is harnessed at a huge geothermal electricity station.

72

Hell's Gate is one of the few parks in Kenya in which you are allowed to walk unguided. The full walk measures some 22km, though most visitors are content to take the waymarked trail (6km there and back), which leads from the park 'Interpretation Centre' (actually just a noticeboard and viewpoint by a car park). This is as far as you can drive without four-wheel drive, and you must park here if you intend walking anywhere in the gorge as there is no space for parking further on. Close by is another volcanic plug known as the Central Rock Tower or Ol Basta. There are good numbers of grazing animals to be seen, and ornithologists will enjoy Hell's Gate as it is a breeding ground for raptors.

LAKE BARINGO

✪✪✪

This beautiful expanse of fresh water provides the best bird-watching in Kenya, with over 450 species recorded here. As you approach the lake you will notice its unusual reddish-pink colour. This is due to the silting effect of the local red topsoil.

The Lake Baringo Club (➤ 104) is the centre of lakeside activities, running boat trips and walking tours. Drop in for a drink on their beautiful lawns and you can't help but see several multicoloured species of birds.

A highlight of a boat trip is feeding the fish eagles. Hippos and crocodiles can also be seen on the lake, and the former come ashore at night, often wandering right up to guests chalets, though there are armed *askaris* (guards) to prevent problems. Excursions also visit the island on the lake, where there is a luxury tented camp.

➕ 28B3
🕐 Daily dawn–dusk
💲 Cheap
↔ Lake Bogoria (➤ 74)

Lake Baringo provides fishing for local people as well as tourism

2B3
PO Box 64, Marigat or
PO Box 53, Kabarnet
328-22068
Expensive
Lake Baringo (➤ 73)

*Pretty in pink – though
you may have to visit
Lake Bogoria to see
flamingos in these
numbers*

LAKE BOGORIA NATIONAL RESERVE ✪✪✪

Bogoria is currently the most colourful lake in Kenya, attracting a million or so of the lesser flamingos which were formerly resident on Lake Nakuru. It's a magnificent sight, though the lake would be worth a visit even without its roseate visitors. Orientation is simple; there's just one road which skirts the western lakeshore.

On the opposite side (no access to here or the lake) is the splendid backdrop of the Siracho escarpment, rising almost sheer for 600m. Towards the end of the road are boiling hot springs, and it is around this area where most of the flamingos gather. You are free to leave your vehicle, though for your own sake do heed the warning signs which tell you where to tread; a spray of scalding steam can break through the thin surface without warning.

The springs are quite a spectacle in their own right; the larger ones blow up to a height of 5m while the rest bubble and brew like so-many witches cauldrons, carving little rivulets of steaming water in the lakeshore.

Two spectacular creatures to keep a look out for are fish eagles and the greater kudu. The former are an unusual sight because Bogoria is so saline; because no fish could live here, the eagles prey on flamingos instead. The handsome, striped greater kudu is rare in Kenya, seen regularly only here and at Marsabit in the north.

LAKE NAIVASHA ✪✪✪

Karen Blixen described Lake Naivasha as 'a paradise on earth' and it's hard to argue. Around the lake is a classic, mature post-volcanic landscape of green humps and bumps with wisps of steam indicating that there is still great energy below the surface.

The lake is best known for its birdlife, with the largest waterfowl population in Kenya and around 340 resident species; fish eagles, goliath herons, storks, kingfishers, flamingos and the rare Verraux's eagle owls are just a few of its larger and more colourful residents. Hippos also live in the waters, and you can take a boat out to visit them, but do keep a safe distance.

➕ 62A3
↔ Hell's Gate National Park (➤ 72–3)

Parts of the margin also provide good game viewing, though there is no reserve or national park designation as all of the land is privately owned. Some of the largest plots now belong to flower farms who export huge quantities to Western Europe and the US.

Because of its proximity to Nairobi (90km south), Lake Naivasha has long been a favourite retreat of the monied classes, and there are some beautiful lakeside holiday homes in the area. Among its most famous residents were Joy Adamson (➤ 72) and Lord Delamere and his notorious Happy Valley set (➤ 76). The focus of interest at Lake Naivasha is along Moi South Lake road (➤ 76). Moi North Lake road is very poorly surfaced and not recommended for driving.

Don't underestimate these lumbering water giants – they can snap a boat in two with their powerful jaws!

A Drive Around the Three Lakes

Dawn at Lake Naivasha

This beautiful drive along the southern shore of Lake Naivasha (➤ 75) includes two smaller satellite lakes. In the dry season you can do this journey in a heavy two-wheel-drive car, but after wet weather you need a four-wheel-drive vehicle.

Lake Naivasha Country Club (➤ 104) is the area's largest concentration of accommodation. It stands in beautiful grounds which are well worth a visit and also provides access to the Crescent Island Sanctuary, a tiny island with excellent bird-watching and surprisingly good game viewing.

After 18km is Elsamere (➤ 72), and a few hundred metres beyond this (on the right) the white building in Moorish style is the infamous Oserian/Djinn Palace, haunt of the Happy Valley set (➤ 78). After another 2.5km the tarmac ends. Turn right here and skirt the beautiful small Oloiden Lake which forms the southeastern tip of Lake Naivasha.

On the far side note the pagoda-like tower, which is a private luxury holiday retreat.

Continue for another 5km, forking right/ straight on by the Kongoni police post. After another 5.5km turn right, continue for 1.5km, then turn right again to enter Crater Lake Sanctuary (➤ 72) and park your car.

Descend the wooden steps to the Crater Lake Camp (➤ 104) for a drink in a magnificent setting and advice on walking in the crater.

Distance
33km

Time
2–3 hours driving time; a full day if you see all the sights

Start point
Lake Naivasha Country Club
➕ 62A3

End point
Crater Lake
➕ 62A3

Lunch
Crater Lake Camp (££–£££)
☎ Via Mythos Ltd 333-569
224826
Elsamere (£)
☎ 0311 21055
(Both must be booked ahead)

LAKE NAKURU NATIONAL PARK ●●●

Lake Nakuru is world famous for its flocks of lesser flamingos, and was created a national park in order to protect them. Unfortunately for the park, in recent years their movements have become rather capricious, coming and going and (at the time of writing) removing themselves mostly to Lake Bogoria (➤ 74). Whether this is merely a cyclical change, in search of new food, or is influenced by other factors (such as pollution) is unclear.

Nakuru is more than just flamingos, however. Over 400 species of birdlife have been recorded here, making it second only to Lake Baringo as the most prolific ornithological site in Kenya. Because the park is relatively small (10km by 25km) and completely fenced it is also a sanctuary for large introduced mammals. White rhinos have been donated by South Africa, and black rhinos have been relocated here from less safe parks in Kenya, bringing the total count to almost 50 altogether. Problem leopards are also sent to Nakuru, and the chances of seeing these rare and elusive animals is better here than in any other park.

You will definitely see waterbucks, buffaloes and warthogs, with zebras and eland (➤ 50–1) a strong possibility. Look out, too, for Rothschild giraffes (➤ 58) introduced from Western Kenya. Lions, also re-introduced to the park, are scarce, and elephants are absent.

✚ 46A2
✉ PO Box 439, Nakuru
☎ 037-41605
▮ Very expensive

Rhino – one of the heavyweights

A Walk on Mount Longonot

Distance
Approx 3km

Time
4–5 hours

Start/end point
Mount Longonot National Park Gate
🕂 62A2
🏛 Park expensive

Lunch
Pack a picnic

The clearest times of year for this climb are January to March and July to October. Climb early in the morning as there is little shade. Because of past security problems you must be escorted by a park ranger.

The climb up the side of the volcano, ascending 576m in altitude, should take around an hour. It's very straightforward, though the final section is quite steep.

The views out over the Rift Valley are wonderful, but the great surprise is looking into the crater. It's like Conan Doyle's *Lost World*, a hidden jungle where, until quite recently, elephants could be seen. You can, in theory, scramble down a steep path to the bottom; it's to the left of the path you have just walked up. This is for experienced scramblers only, though, and remember there are buffalo still down below!

Walk in an anticlockwise direction around the rim as the climb to the highest part is easier to negotiate this way.

It isn't far (around 1km), but the path is narrow and crumbly and you'll want to stop quite often to enjoy the changing views, so allow the best part of three hours. Note, on the north side of the cone, a small 'parasitic cone', formed by escaping magma when the main vent of the volcano was blocked by cooled lava. Next to the highest point is a small plateau where you can stop for some well-earned refreshment.

The descent takes around 30 minutes.

Did you know ?

Lake Naivasha was one of the first places to be settled by the British and became the home of the notorious hard-drinking, drug-taking, wife-swapping, hell-raising 'Happy Valley' set. Many of the antics of this group of titled and aristocratic settlers centred on Oserian (also known as the Djinn Palace or Gin Palace) on the shores of the lake (▶ 76). Their high jinks ended in murder and suicide as related in the book and film White Mischief.

MOUNT LONGONOT NATIONAL PARK ✪✪

Created around a million years ago, Mount Longonot, at 2,776m, is the youngest and highest of the Rift Valley volcanoes. It has an almost perfect circular cone about 1km in diameter and is an unmissable sight from the viewpoints on the A104 Nairobi road. It is also an excellent place to stretch your legs (▶ 78).

✚ 62A2
🕐 Daily dawn–dusk
💰 Expensive
🔄 Hell's Gate National Park
(▶ 73), Lake Naivasha
(▶ 75)

NYAHURURU (THOMSON'S FALLS) ✪✪

Set high in the north of the Aberdares, the town of Nyahururu used to be known by the name of its famous natural attraction, Thomson's Falls. The falls thunder into a gorge 72m below, and viewed from Thomson's Falls Lodge, across the gorge, are an impressive and very photogenic sight. You do have to run the gauntlet of a mini-village of souvenir sellers, however. A pleasant, if slippery, 10-minute walk to the bottom of the falls is worth while, but be careful. The lawn of the lodge is a pleasant place for refreshments (▶ 99).

There's nothing in the town of Nyahururu to distract visitors.

✚ 62A4

Thomson's Falls, 'discovered' in 1883 by the intrepid young Scottish explorer, Joseph Thomson

Food & Drink

If you are visiting Kenya on a package holiday the probability is that all your meals are inclusive and will comprise all-you-can-eat buffets of mostly familiar Western-style dishes. All is not

lost, however. The standard of such food is often good and some African or at least African-style dishes will be offered. Some hotels also have special African nights where you can sample the dishes mentioned below.

Meat Dishes

The favourite Kenyan feast, *nyama choma*, consists of barbecued meat, which typically includes chicken, goat, beef and mutton. A limited number of outlets also offer game – zebra (which is surprisingly tasty), gazelle, eland, hartebeest, ostrich and even crocodile.

Vegetable Dishes

For the majority of Kenyans, meat is a luxury. The staple vegetable stew is *githeri*, which can include just about anything – maize, red beans,

Top: *buffet food is the norm in Kenyan hotels and lodges*
Above: *nyama choma (grilled meat) is always popular with visitors*

potatoes, carrots, kale/spinach, tomatoes, onions etc. Vegetarians beware, there may be a little meat in it, too. *Irio* is a vegetable mash of peas, maize and potatoes. *Ugali* is a thick maize meal porridge – pure stodge, as bland in taste as its white appearance. *Matoke* is mashed green plantains, not unlike mashed potatoes in taste.

In international hotels and restaurants salads are copious and there is usually a choice of Indian vegetarian dishes, too.

Fish and Seafood

Tilapia, usually battered, is a sweet, tasty, freshwater fish. Another lake fish is Nile perch, cooked in a variety of ways. Smoked tuna is a common starter. Sailfish is sometimes smoked as a starter, and also served battered. The best fish and seafood dishes are to be found on the coast where Swahili cooking combines crab, 'lobster' (nearly always crayfish) and prawns with coconut milk, ginger, tamarind, chillies and lime juice to delicious effect. Curries are also common.

Fruit

Pineapple, mango, papaya, water melon, banana and passion fruit are staple items on the buffet table.

Drinks

The ubiquitous alcoholic drink is the fairly bland Tusker lager. It was named by a brewer in the 1920s in honour of his brother, who was killed in an elephant stampede. For a bit more taste, upgrade to Tusker Premium. As bizarre as it may sound, in many establishments you must ask for cold beer, otherwise it may be served warm.

If you order wine there is a high probability it will be South African. The only area to produce wine in Kenya is Lake Naivasha. Some of it is very good, so do try it. The only other wine that you may see, though it is not usually on the menu, is papaya wine. This is usually euphemistically described as 'an acquired taste'. After dinner try the national coffee liqueur, Kenya Gold.

Beware: some parts of the coast adhere strictly to Moslem teaching and are 'dry' – in Lamu town only two establishments serve alcohol. Soft drinks are referred to generically as soda.

Top: *Giriama home cooking*
Above: *Mombasa Market produce*

Western Kenya

Western Kenya is virtually untouched by tourism. Its most famous place, Lake Victoria, is something of an anti-climax, though still a magnetic draw. The Kakamega Forest, Mount Elgon and the Saiwa Swamp are attractions which, but for their isolation, would draw significant numbers of visitors. In fact, the latter two are only three to four hours drive from Lake Baringo, along a route which takes in the C51, one of the best kept and most scenic roads in all Kenya.

Much of Western Kenya is a rewarding region for driving, with good roads looking on to rolling hills of lush natural vegetation and cultivated fields set on steep terraces.

'There lay the end of our pilgrimage – a glistening bay of the great lake ... softly veiled and rendered weirdly indistinct by a dense haze. The view could not be called picturesque, though it was certainly pleasing.'

JOSEPH THOMSON
(on reaching Lake Victoria)
Through Masailand (1883)

28A3
Kenya Wildlife Service
District Warden, PO Box
879, Kakamega
331-20425
Free, but contribution to
forest conservation funds
requested

Rondo Retreat Centre
331 30268

KAKAMEGA FOREST RESERVE ✪✪

This is the last surviving tropical rain forest in Kenya, and is a renowned sanctuary for birds, butterflies and primates. It is best visited during the rainy season (April to July) when the flowers are at their most beautiful.

Brilliantly coloured turacos, noisy hornbills and around 350 other species of birds make Kakamega Forest an ornithologist's paradise, though viewing is not easy so ask the knowledgeable park guides to accompany you. Often more visible are the forest primates; black-and-white colobus, the white-bearded de Brazza monkey and rare species such as blue monkey, olive baboon and red-tailed monkey.

There are two bird-watching trails; one in the north, by the Kenya Wildlife Service Forest Station – where there are *bandas* (huts) and camping, and one in the south, at the Isecheno Forest Station, where there are two small accommodations.

28A3
Kisumu (► below)

KERICHO ✪

This is the tea centre of Kenya, which is the world's third largest producer after India and Sri Lanka. In keeping with the neatly aligned rows of tea plants and the area's regimented colonial history, the centre of Kericho is (by Kenyan standards) also orderly and tidy.

The best place to stay, or just to sample a cup of tea, is the Tea Hotel (► 104). Disappointingly, organised tours of the tea plantations have recently ceased operating, but the Tea Hotel is a good place to ask about the possibilty of an informal tour.

28A3
Kisumu Museum, Nairobi
Road, PO Box 1779
35-40803
Daily 8:30–6
Cheap
Kericho (► above)

Impala Wildlife Sanctuary
Dawn–dusk
Free

KISUMU ✪✪

With a population of over 160,000, this is the third largest city in Kenya and the main town on Lake Victoria. It was founded in 1901 as the inland railhead of the Uganda/East Africa Railway (► 57) and flourished as a trading port with Tanzania and Uganda. Over the past three decades it has suffered badly as a result of the break-up of the old East African Community trade and transport alliance, and Uganda's troubles. Tourists are a novelty here, but Kisumu has enough sights to occupy a day.

The market, by the bus station, is the most colourful in Western Kenya, and a short walk along the Nairobi Road is the Kisumu Museum. This is probably the best provincial museum in the country, with a good display of ethno-graphic artefacts. There are some curious stuffed exhibits too, such as a lion attacking a wildebeest, and a record 189kg Nile perch pulled from the lake.

For wildlife viewing head just south of town to the **Impala Wildlife Sanctuary**, where you may see rare sitatunga deer (► 90), alongside the common impala. Close by is the Hippo Point Sanctuary where you can watch these lumbering giants feeding – the boatmen will take you up close – and enjoy the sunset. Check the local security situation before visiting.

Also near by is the traditional fishing village of Dunga, where there are more hippos and birds to view while afloat.

From the fields of Kenya to the tea cups of the world

Birdlife

Kenya is the best place in Africa for bird-watching with over 1,000 species reliably recorded. Only Zaire has more birds, but its sites are less accessible and its political situation is unstable. The reason for such an abundance of birdlife lies partly in the diversity of habitats. Within a relatively small distance you can find mountains, highland and lowland forest, tropical rain forest, freshwater and soda lakes, savannah, desert and coast. A pair of binoculars is essential equipment and a copy of Collins *Field Guide to the Birds of East Africa* is also recommended.

Savannah

The world's largest bird, ostriches can weigh up to 150kg

There's always a lull when big-game spotting, so use the time to scan the bush for birdlife. The biggest of all the birds is the 2m-tall ostrich which roams the open grass-lands in small family groups. The males are black and

white, the females dusty brown. Ostriches are flightless, but they can run at speeds of up to 50kph and give a mean defensive kick (you'll never see them with their head in the sand!).

Perched on top of acacia and thorn trees are vultures' nests. The most common species is the white-backed vulture, with a wingspan of over 2m. The other ubiquitous scavenger is the marabou stork which is equally at home on urban refuse tips. It stands over 2m tall, but with its bald pink head, and thin legs cloaked by black tailcoat-like wings, it cuts a shabby figure. By contrast, the leggy, crested secretary bird has a very dapper grey-black appearance, with quill feathers on the back of its head.

Other favourites include speckled mousebirds (with their distinctive long ribbon-like tails), colourful bee-eaters, tiny jewel-like sunbirds and, around the lodges, the aptly named superb starling, brilliantly coloured in iridescent blue/black with beady yellow/orange eyes.

Top: *two of Kenya's less endearing birds, marabou storks and white-beaked vultures*
Above: *the elegant fish eagle in action on Lake Victoria*

Water Birds

Pink carpets of flamingos have become a trademark of Kenya. Alongside them, almost forgotten, are white clouds of pelicans. Another favourite of the Rift Valley lakes is the tall, handsome black, white and chestnut African fish eagle (► 74).

An unusual bird is the hammerkop, whose name means hammer head and is self-explanatory on sight. Kingfishers usually come in malachite (multicoloured) or pied (monochrome) varieties.

Herons, cranes, cormorants, darters and yellow-billed storks perch on the shoreline; ducks, geese and moorhens float across the surface; ibis and sandpipers stab at the shallows. Kenya's national bird, the elegant crowned crane, is often seen in marshy areas.

Forest Birds

Turacos and hornbills, both large and distinctive species of bird, are the stars of the forest. Turacos are often brilliantly coloured, while hornbills, named after their long, heavy bills, are usually black and white.

✚ 28A3
↔ Kisumu (➤ 84–5)

LAKE VICTORIA ✪

Lake Victoria is the largest body of fresh water in Africa. Its very name conjures up romance. The first European to sight the lake was John Hanning Speke in 1858, while seeking the mysterious source of the White Nile. He named it Victoria and on little more than a hunch declared that this was indeed the river's source. He was ridiculed, only to be vindicated 17 years later by H M Stanley.

The lake is vast – at 67,483sq km it is bigger than many countries – though only just over 5 per cent of it is found in Kenya (the rest is in Tanzania and Uganda).

During the late 19th century, Lake Victoria attracted huge interest in Europe as each of the colonial powers (England, Germany and France) plotted in vain a navigable route along the Nile to the Mediterranean.

Yet despite its historical resonance, it's a disappointment to most visitors. Scenically it's usually dull, a steely grey colour for much of the year because of persistent haze and cloud. It is a potentially serious health

When the boats come in – Luo craft on Lake Victoria

hazard, home to bilharzia parasites and malarial mosquitoes, and the lake itself is under threat from various environmental dangers. The latest is the water hyacinth, a floating weed (also found on Lake Naivasha), which eventually kills all lake life by removing the oxygen.

MOUNT ELGON NATIONAL PARK ✪✪✪

Situated right on the Uganda border, Mount Elgon is known as the 'loneliest park in Kenya'. It is also one of its most impressive, still very wild, with large areas of untouched forest. At over 4,300m, it is the second highest mountain in Kenya after Mount Kenya. It attracts relatively few climbers, though some of its highest slopes make excellent hiking country.

Visitors with less time, but a modicum of fitness, should aim for Endebess Bluff (2,563m) to enjoy the marvellous views. Another excellent vantage point is Elephant Platform (accessible by road). Sadly, the elephants are no longer visible from here, decimated by

paochers in the 1980s. An estimated 400 elephants remain in the park, though the thick forest makes them difficult to spot. Their most famous gathering place is Kitum Cave. This is the largest and most famous of Mount Elgon's several caves, extending 200m back into the mountain. Take a powerful flashlight in order to see the tusk marks which indicate where the elephants forage for salt deposits. They only come at night, but at any time of day or night there are hundreds of thousands of screeching bats in here, too. The park's other large cave is the Makingeni, its entrance draped by a curtain of waterfall.

Other animals on the mountain include buffalo, antelope, colobus monkey, blue monkey and leopard.

SAIWA SWAMP ✪✪
(► 90, WALK)

✚ 28A3
☎ 325-20329
⏰ Daily dawn–dusk
💷 Expensive
↔ Saiwa Swamp (► 90)
❓ Recommended guide, Tony Mills Safaris, ☎ 02-571647 (via Bush Homes) (► 101)

✚ 28A3

A Walk Around Saiwa Swamp

Distance
3.5–8.5km

Time
2–5 hours

Start/end point
Saiwa Swamp Park Entrance
✛ 28A3

Lunch
There are no facilities, so take a packed lunch

Measuring less than 3sq km, this is Kenya's smallest park and the only one dedicated to walking trails. A mixture of jungle and swamp, it was created as an environment for the rare semi-aquatic sitatunga deer and provides delightful shaded waymarked trails with treetop viewing platforms. It's also excellent for bird-watching. Park your car and ask the wardens where is currently the best place to see the sitatunga. Come early in the morning or late afternoon for the best opportunities.

Depending on their advice, take the sign to the left, 'Observation Platform Trails'. After around 100m there is a fork marked 'Nature Trail' 7km (straight on); 'Observation Platforms' (right). Go right and cross the rickety boardwalk.

Stop here for a while and you may spot a sitatunga at close quarters. Don't be surprised to see local people as well, crossing the boardwalk.

Cross the boardwalk and turn right at the sign 'Platform No 5 845m'.

This is a lovely walk through the forest with the swamp to your right. Keep peering through the trees for signs of sitatunga and also kingfishers, and look above for hornbills and turacos (➤ 87). The most prominent inhabitant of the swamp is the crested crane, also conspicuous by its honking call.

Climb to the top of Platform No 5, a Robinson Crusoe–like tree-house with superb views. Walk back the way you came (845m), then continue straight on to Platform No 4 (a further 780m).

This is a three-storey, man-made platform, offering views into a different part of the swamp.

From here return the way you came to the car park (approximately 1km), or if you want to see primates, contine ahead to pick up the Nature Trail.

Several types of monkey live along here – colobus, blue, vervet and the mandarin-faced, white-bearded de Brazza's.

This trail brings you back around the swamp to the car-park.

Where To...

The Coast

Prices
Approximate prices for a three-course meal for one person are shown by the pound symbol:

£   = under 500 KSh
££ = 500–1,000 KSh
£££ = over 1,000 KSh

All establishments are open daily for lunch and dinner unless otherwise stated.

Mombasa

Le Bistro (££)
Excellent meeting point right by the famous tusks, open all day, serving a wide range of international food in a very pleasant relaxed atmosphere.
✉ **Moi Avenue** ☎ **No tel bookings**

Hard Rock Café (££)
A safe bet for a good American-international lunch after shopping; conveniently close to Fort Jesus and the old town. Lively in the evenings.
✉ **Nkrumah Road** ☎ **011-222221**

Mombasa Coffee House (££)
The official High Street outlet of the Kenyan coffee board, so quality is guaranteed. Try their house speciality – pineapple pie. A good place to rest awhile.
✉ **Moi Avenue** ☎ **No tel**

Recoda (£)
The best Swahili food in old Mombasa. Frustratingly closed at lunchtime but worth the evening taxi ride and adventure into the Old Town if you are close by in Nyali. Try to arrive by 7PM to avoid missing out on the most popular dishes.
✉ **Nyeri Street, Old Town** ☎ **No tel** ⏰ **Dinner only; closed Mon & Ramadan**

Shehnai (£££)
Charming Indian restaurant serving excellent Mughlai and tandoori dishes in an ornate incense-filled atmosphere.
✉ **Fatemi House, Maungano Street (off Moi Avenue, behind the Hotel Splendid)** ☎ **011-312492** ⏰ **Closed Mon**

North of Mombasa

Carneval (£££)
A good place to escape your hotel for a special night out. Seafood and game specialities, Japanese sushi dishes (confirm in advance), plus good music, all with a romantic view over-looking Tudor Creek. There's a choice of bars and a piano lounge too.
✉ **Next to Nyali Bridge (complimentary transport to local hotels)** ☎ **011-474040**

Minar (£££)
A branch of the reliable and popular small Indian chain of restaurants. This one specialises in Mughlai dishes.
✉ **Links Road (next to Nyali Golf Club)** ☎ **011-472136**

Nyali Beach Hotel (£££)
Regarded as the best hotel food in the area with a good choice of restaurants with rotating menus. Make sure you sample African and Swahili dishes.
✉ **Nyali Beach** ☎ **011-471861**

Pirates (££–£££)
A popular bar and restaurant, particularly if you have kids in tow (➤ 111).
✉ **Kenyatta Beach** ☎ **011-486441**

Tamarind Restaurant (£££)
Often regarded as serving the best seafood in all Kenya, and with a great view looking over the water to Mombasa. The prawns piti piri, chilli crab and lobster Swahili are outstanding and the combined seafood platter (which is surprisingly good value) is a must. One for romantics (➤ 113, Tamarind Dhow trip).

✉ Nyali (signposted from Nyali Bridge) ☎ 011-471747

Ziga Restaurant (£–££)

Top-quality authentic Swahili food with matching entertainment under a cavernous *makuti* (palm thatch) shelter. Go for the all-inclusive Swahili barbecue. Friendly staff and very relaxed atmosphere.

✉ Bombolulu Workshops and Cultural Centre ☎ 011-471704 🕐 Lunch only Mon–Sat. Closed Sun

Diani Beach
Ali Barbour's Cave Restaurant (£££)

Enjoy the very best Kenyan seafood (crab salad marinated with lime and chilli, jumbo prawns in a mild pili pili sauce) and French cuisine (chicken breast filled with mushroom mousse). A magical setting inside a romantic naturally formed coral cave open to the stars (a sliding roof keeps diners dry on rainy nights). Extensive wine list.

✉ Diani Beach road, 3km south of the main junction. Free transport to Diani Beach hotels ☎ 0127-2163 🕐 Dinner only

Boko Boko (££)

A bit of a trek (at the far end of the Diani Beach road), but worth it to find this charming garden restaurant specialising in Seychelles cooking at very reasonable prices.

✉ Diani Beach road, 9.5km south of the main junction

Forty Thieves Beach Bar (£–££)

Lively, popular meeting place by day and night, serving snacks and a 'special

evening menu' (➤ 112).

✉ Diani Beach, off main road 3km south of the main junction ☎ 0127-2033

Gallos (££)

Good international and Kenyan food on an eclectic menu, popular with tourists and local *wazungus* (whites).

✉ Diani Shopping Centre, Diani Beach road (1km south of the main junction) ☎ 0127-3150

Maharani (£££)

You can't miss the imposing Taj Mahal-style building and the food is pretty impressive too, particularly their tandoori specialities.

✉ Diani Beach Road (2.5km south of the main junction) ☎ 0127-2439 🕐 Closed Wed

Nomad's (£–£££)

By day, relax at one of the original Diani Beach beach bars, with good basic food and sand between your toes looking out on to one of the most popular stretches of the beach; by night, enjoy gourmet cooking on a terrace in the main restaurant by the hotel reception. Friday nights are particularly lively and Sunday features a curry buffet with jazz. Be aware, however, that you must order your drinks separately from your food.

✉ Diani Beach road (5km south of the main junction) ☎ 0127-2155

Vulcanos (£££)

The best Italian food on Diani Beach, albeit at a price, and in a rather formal atmosphere. Air-conditioning.

✉ Diani Beach road (6.8km south of the main junction) ☎ 0127-2004

Ramadan

At Ramadan (➤ 116) most 'local' restaurants (ie those not mostly dependent on tourists) will close during the day, and some will remain closed during the evening. Note, too, that this type of restaurant may not serve alcohol. Most of Lamu is 'dry'.

Medicine
Probably the most potent drink you will come across in Kenya is *dawa* (Swahili for medicine). This is a cocktail of vodka, white rum, lime juice and honey, and is traditionally served on dhow trips.

Lamu Island

Bush Gardens (£)
Popular basic seafood and grills restaurant in a pleasant al fresco setting. Food is cheap and filling, but quality is disappointing. Their garlic bread is worth a try but avoid the 'lobster' (crayfish).

✉ **Waterfront, next to Petley's Inn** ☎ **No tel**

Hapa Hapa (£)
Similar format to its neighbour Bush Gardens (see above) though even more cheap and cheerful. You can (discreetly) bring your own booze here.

✉ **Waterfront, next to Petley's Inn** ☎ **No tel**

Lamu Palace (£££)
Certainly the poshest place to eat in Lamu town and regarded as serving the best seafood too; the all-you-can-eat buffet is very good value.

✉ **Waterfront** ☎ **0121-33272**

Peponi Hotel (££–£££)
Excellent grilled dishes in a cosy garden enclosed by stone walls reminiscent of an old ruined Swahili settlement. The perfect place to break a hard day's sunbathing on Shela Beach.

✉ **Shela Beach** ☎ **0121-33154** 🕐 **Lunchtimes only, dining room only open to residents in evening**

Petley's Inn (££–£££)
The downstairs bar of this long-established and fairly basic watering hole is the best place for a beer and people-watching in Lamu. With recent improvements to the rooftop restaurant (closed for refurbishment at time of writing) it may well become a very good place to eat, too.

✉ **Waterfront, next to ferry jetty** ☎ **0121-33107**

Rumours at Baraka (£–££)
By far the most civilised place in Lamu town for a coffee (they even have *cappuccino*) accompanied by very tasty cakes and ice-creams. Sooner or later every European gravitates here. Good pizzas and a limited range of other meals, too. Charming small courtyard garden with newspapers provided. Service is friendly and laid-back but can be slow.

✉ **Harambee Avenue (south end)**

Serena Vegetarian Restaurant (££)
Formerly the Yoghurt Inn, with a long tradition of serving the best vegetarian meals on Lamu. They also do seafood and (of course) home-made yoghurt.

✉ **Harambee Avenue (north end)**

Malindi

Ai Pescatori (££)
Good for pizzas, cooked in wood-fired oven; also serves the usual range of pasta and other Italian dishes.

✉ **Harambee Road (waterfront), near the turn-off for the Vasco da Gama monument** ☎ **0123-31198**

The Driftwood Club (££–£££)
A perennial favourite with Anglo Kenyans and Malindi regulars. Their barbecues and Sunday curry buffet are both hotly recommended.

✉ **2km south of town** ☎ **0123-20155**

I Love Pizza (££)
Don't let the silly name put you off, one taste and you will probably love their pizzas too. The seafood and pasta dishes are also good, and the surroundings are pleasant.

✉ Harambee Road (waterfront) ☎ 0123-20672

Malindi Sea Fishing Club (££)
Reasonably priced seafood and grills with fine sea views. It's worth popping in just for a drink and to see the latest deep-sea trophies; in 1997 they hauled in one of the largest great white sharks ever to be found in these waters.

✉ Harambee Road (waterfront) ☎ 0123-30550 (temporary club membership costs $1)

Palm Garden (£–££)
A basic bar-restaurant with prostitutes and hustlers at the front, but don't let that put you off – there's a pleasant eating area at the back serving good seafood and curries. Live music on Fridays.

◐ Harambee Road (next to the Standard Bank) ☎ No tel

Surahi (££–£££)
Probably the best Indian restaurant in Malindi.

✉ Off Harambee Road, on road by side of Barclays Bank ☎ 0123-20911

Vera Cruz (££)
A Portuguese theme-restaurant recalling the days of Vasco da Gama and subsequent Portuguese traders. It's worth coming here for a drink at least (there's a pool, too, for a lunchtime dip).

✉ Beachfront, Harambee Road, next to Casino ☎ 0123-20674

Wasini Island
Wasini Island Restaurant (£££)
A genuine desert-island setting with the sand between your toes and *makuti* (palm-thatch) above your head. The traditional meal comprises marinated fish and coconut, fabulous-tasting whole crabs steamed in ginger, followed by barbecued fish with Swahili sauce, accompanied by coconut rice and chapatis. Wash it all down with a large choice of wines and cocktails. Don't worry if you're not on the snorkelling trip (► 25) – you can still eat here.

✉ Wasini Island (call the restaurant who will arrange a boat from Shimoni – ► 44) ☎ 0127-2331

Watamu
Hemingway's (£££)
Excellent food and particularly pleasant at lunch time, with some very good-value dishes and an idyllic view over Turtle Bay. Service can be slow when busy.

✉ Turtle Bay ☎ 0122-32624 ◐ Closed May, Jun

Ocean Sport (£££)
Adjacent to Hemingway's (see above), serving an excellent seafood lunch buffet on Sundays and various other special nights (including curries, Chinese food). Nice laid-back atmosphere.

✉ Turtle Bay ☎ 0123-32008

Sunday Best
Many hotels feature a special Sunday lunchtime curry buffet at a very reasonable price. If you are not on this circuit (ie staying in Kenya on a bed-and-breakfast or a self-catering basis) this is usually a good time to visit.

Nairobi & Environs

Restaurant Capital
Nairobi is the restaurant capital of East Africa. You can find almost every kind of food here, and with large ex-pat communities from many parts of the world it is usually authentic and high quality.

Nairobi City Centre

African Heritage (££)
Relax after shopping here (► 108) with traditional African food, accompanied by dancers and musicians. Friday is Ethiopian night, which means the opportunity to sample some unusual and very tasty dishes.
🖂 **Kenyatta Avenue** ☎ **02-333507**

Akasaka (£££)
The city's best Japanese restaurant, famous for its reasonably priced lunchboxes.
🖂 **Standard Street (next to The Pub)** ☎ **02-333948**

Bobbé's Bistro (£££)
This small intimate French restaurant has been a favourite with ex-pats and serious foodies for over 30 years.
🖂 **Cianda House, Koinange Street** ☎ **02-336952** Ⓓ **Dinner only Sat. Closed Sun**

Buffalo Bill's
This sleazy watering hole with a woman in every covered wagon is a Nairobi institution. Single men don't stay single too long. Good fun for broad-minded groups. Not recommended for food.
🖂 **Heron Court Hotel, Milimani Road** ☎ **02-720740**

Le Château (£££)
Nairobi's only rooftop garden, serving excellent international cuisine. Dinner dances at weekends.
🖂 **Intercontinental Hotel, City Hall Way** ☎ **02-335550**

The Delamere Terrace, Norfolk Hotel (££–£££)
The place to watch the new arrivals and safari comings and goings in Nairobi. Food not reputed to be as good as it was, and service can be slow. The bar at the far end is a popular meeting place for locals and ex-pats.
🖂 **Harry Thuku Road** ☎ **02-335422**

Dhaba (££)
One of the best north Indian restaurants in the city, also with a *nyama choma* (► 80) dining room.
🖂 **Keekorok Road, at top end of Tom Mboya Street** ☎ **02-334862**

Flame Tree Bar, Pan-Afric Hotel
A popular and often lively drinking hole for ex-pats and more affluent locals, with a large outdoor terrace shaded by flame trees.
🖂 **Kenyatta Avenue** ☎ **02-720822**

Ibis Grill, Norfolk Hotel (£££)
A winner of the 'Kenya Restaurant of the Year' award, serving superb French nouvelle cuisine in a beautiful dining-room.
🖂 **Harry Thuku Road** ☎ **02-335422**

Iqbal Hotel (£)
Cheap and cheerful, serving traditional Indian and African food, popular with budget travellers.
🖂 **Latema Road, near the Odeon Cinema** ☎ **02-220914**

Kariakor Market (£)
A good opportunity to sample *nyama choma* (► 80) and African street food with the locals at rock-bottom prices. Choose items which look freshly cooked or are cooked in front of you.
🖂 **Racecourse Road**

Mayur (£–££)
Superb South Indian vegetarian cuisine with a bargain buffet that makes it worth missing our breakfast and/or lunch. In a dodgy part of town so take a taxi.
✉ **Supreme Hotel, Keekorok Road** ☎ **02-225241**

Minar (£££)
Reliable small Indian chain, specialising in Mughlai cuisine and recommended for their tandoori dishes and buffet lunches.
✉ **Banda Street (branches also at Sarit Street, Westlands and the Ya Ya Centre, Hurlingham)** ☎ **02-330168**

Red Bull (£££)
Long-established, rather old-fashioned Swiss-German-style establishment, serving some of the best steaks and game meat in town.
✉ **First Floor, Transnational Plaza, Mama Ngina Street** ☎ **02-228045 (bookings only taken for Sat, Sun dinner)**

Rickshaw Restaurant (££–£££)
Highly regarded Cantonese food in the heart of the city.
✉ **Fedha Towers, corner of Muindi Mbingu Street and Standard Street** ☎ **02-223604** 🕐 **Daily**

Sagret Hotel £
A real local's nyama choma (► 80), down-to-earth, friendly. Much less choice than the famous Carnivore (► 98), but also at a fraction of the price of the price.
✉ **Milimani Road** ☎ **No tel**

Shogun (£££)
High quality Japanese food, in a less formal atmosphere than that of Akasaka (► 96)

and cheaper too. Book a table in one of the traditional rooms. Extensive menu, including excellent sashimi.
✉ **Argwings Kodhek Road** ☎ **02-716080** 🕐 **Closed Sun**

Tamarind (£££)
Sister restaurant to the famous Tamarind in Mombasa (► 92), serving the best seafood in Nairobi.
✉ **National Bank Building, Aga Khan Walk, off Harambee Avenue or Haile Selassie Avenue** ☎ **02-338959** 🕐 **Closed Sun lunch**

Thorn Tree Café (££)
Nairobi's most famous meeting point – the thorn tree in the centre of the café was once the message board for all East Africa's travellers – and a welcome safe haven from the city hustle and bustle for food. Note – service can be slow and between 11 and 2, and 5 and 7 you must order food.
✉ **New Stanley Hotel, Kimathi Street** ☎ **02-333233**

Toona Tree (££–£££)
This pleasant al fresco restaurant is nominally Italian but features an interesting and eclectic menu, including smorgasbord and good seafood, and has a playground for children. Resident band five nights a week.
✉ **International Casino complex, Museum Hill** ☎ **02-742600** 🕐 **Closed Mon**

La Trattoria (££–£££)
Probabaly the best traditional Italian food in town; always very popular.
✉ **Corner of Wabera Street and Kaunda Street** ☎ **02-340855**

Local Snacks
In local bars and cafés you will probably see sambusas (samosas) and mandazi. The former is a savoury envelope of spicy minced meat or vegetables, the latter is a cake, tasting rather like an unsweetened or semi-sweet doughnut and is baked daily. Both are triangular in shape and deep fried and are best eaten soon after cooking, mandazi by 10AM at the latest! The ubiquitous street food is grilled corn on the cob.

Colonial Presence

The old colonial presence is still strong in Karen, most notably in the Karen Country Club, and also around Westlands, wher the most famous establishment is the Muthaiga Club. If you're in Nairobia on business, or indeed for any length of time, it's worth trying to get an entrée into these hallowed portals – for a meal or just a drink. You'll need to find a friendly ex-pat who is a member.

Nairobi Environs

African Heritage Centre (££)

The same high quality traditional African menu as served in Nairobi (► 96), also occasionally accompanied by dancers and musicians.

✉ **Libra House, Mombasa Road (Libra House is 7km from the city centre; shuttle buses depart four times a day from the African Heritage shop on Kenyatta Avenue)** ☎ 02-554547

The Carnivore (£££)

Nairobi's most famous *nyama choma* joint (► 80), and frequently nominated as the best of its kind in all Africa. The Carnivore is a colourful, boisterous tourist trap where great hunks of meat are presented on large sword-like skewers and carved at the table. What's on offer varies (see the blackboard) but typically includes eland, crocodile, gazelle, ostrich and zebra, as well as domesticated offerings such as chicken, beef, offal and sausages. The quality of the meat is invariably good and portions are never-ending – so pace yourself! It's good fun if you're with a lively group and in the right place. Ask for a table in the same (front) room as the barbecue pit. Service is not always up to scratch. Dance off your excess at the Simba Saloon. Reservations are advisable.

✉ **Off Langata Road** ☎ 02-501775

Charlie's (£)

The biggest disappointment of a visit to the Karen Blixen House is that there are no refreshments. Don't worry, though, as Charlie's, a few hundred metres away, will take care of you. Adjacent is the Swede House which markets itself as the Karen Blixen Coffee Garden and was the residence of a Swede who was one of Blixen's coffee estate owners.

✉ **Telephone or ask at the Karen Blixen House for directions** ☎ 02-882508 🕐 10-5:30; closed Mon

The Horseman (£–£££)

Everything from pub-grub to gourmet food; a perfect lunchstop on the Karen Blixen Museum circuit (► 59) or the place to come for a special night out. Snack in the garden at any time – in the evening you can enjoy the frog's chorus – or splash out on a top-quality, full-blown meal in the attractive colonial-style dining-rooms. The menu is full of interesting Kenyan-international dishes such as Zanzibari fish and coconut soup. You may also like to visit the mock-Tudor bar where you will probably find ex-pats knocking back the Tuskers.

✉ **Corner of Ngong Road and Langata Road** ☎ 02-882782

Le Restaurant (£££)

Enjoy a day at the races then blow your winnings in style on what is probably the best French haute cuisine in Kenya. Even if your horse hasn't come in, it's still worth a drink in the attractive bar area, decorated with huge Lamu chests and antique carpets. Booking is essential.

✉ **Nairobi Racecourse, Ngong Road** ☎ 02-561002

Rest of Kenya

Central Highlands and Rift Valley

Aberdare Country Club (£££)

Enjoy a lunchtime buffet on the terrace overlooking the Aberdares or a romantic evening meal in the wooden panelled old colonial dining-room.

✉ Mweiga ☎ 0171-55620

The Kentmere Club (£££)

Superb international gourmet food with the emphasis on French cuisine. There's a re-creation of an old English pub here too. Beautiful gardens to relax in.

✉ Old Limuru road ☎ 0154-41053

Mount Kenya Safari Club (£££)

Rub shoulders with the rich and famous over a wonderful buffet lunch or come in the evening for a seven-course extravaganza.

✉ Near Nanyuki ☎ 0176-22960 ❓ Tie no longer required but smart-casual dress essential (no shorts or jeans)

Outspan Hotel (£££)

Excellent buffet lunch and lovely gardens in which to stroll afterwards.

✉ Near Nyeri ☎ 0171-2424

Thomson's Falls Lodge (££)

Lunch on the lawns before walking to the foot of the Falls or doing battle with the souvenir hawkers. It's not gourmet food, but it is a nice setting.

✉ Nyahururu ☎ 0365-22006

Lake Naivasha

La Belle Inn (££–£££)

A long-established and highly recommended restaurant, serving some inventive dishes. Try their Naivasha bisque, made with the best bits from the lake.

✉ Moi Avenue, Naivasha ☎ 0311-21007

Crater Lake Camp (£££)

Cordon Bleu cooking in a perfect setting in your own secret world (➤ 72).

✉ Crater Lake Sanctuary, Lake Naivasha ☎ Via Mythos Ltd 333-569 224826

Elsamere Conservation Centre (£–££)

Visit the former home of Joy Adamson for a traditional afternoon tea or a buffet lunch. Either way, these lovely lawns on the shores of Lake Naivasha provide an idyllic setting (➤ 72).

✉ Lake Naivasha ☎ 0311-21055. Tea served at 4PM, lunch must be booked ahead ⏱ Open during the day only

Western Kenya

Dunga Refreshments (££)

A picturesque spot on Lake Victoria, ideal for a local snack or a proper meal, with an extensive menu featuring vegetarian options and fish from the lake.

✉ Hippo Point, Kisumu ☎ 0354-2529

Kitale Club (££)

This old colonial establish-ment is a good bet for English and Indian dishes.

✉ Kitale-Eldoret road, Kitale ☎ 0325-20030

The Tea Hotel (££)

A good stop for the ubiquitous cup of tea on the terrace overlooking their lovely grounds. Serves reliable Anglo-Indian food.

✉ PO Box 75, Moi Highway, Kericho ☎ 0361-3004

Going Native

Outside of Nairobi, Lake Naivasha and the coastal resorts there are relatively few restaurants that cater for visitors. The small, often ramshackle roadside establishments that you see bearing the name *hoteli* are in fact local bar-restaurants. If you eat at one of these (very few Westerners do) the safest option hygiene-wise is food which is freshly grilled in front of you.

The Coast & Southern Game Parks

Prices
Approximate prices for a double room per night, high season, shown by the pound symbol (in higher class establishments hotel prices are quoted in dollars):

£ = under $70
££ = $70–150
£££ = over $150

HB/FB means tariff includes half board (breakfast and dinner *or* lunch) or full board (breakfast, dinner *and* lunch)

Mombasa (North)

Mombasa Whitesands (£££)

A large rather impersonal hotel devoted mostly to package-holidays, but attractively laid out in extensive grounds and with good facilities, including three swimming pools. Rooms vary so make sure you get one of the newly renovated type. The hotel's speciality seafood restaurant is highly rated.

✉ Bamburi Beach, PO Box 90173 ☎ 011-485926, fax 011-485652. Reservations through Sarova Hotels (➤ 101)

Nyali Beach Hotel (£££)

Often touted as the best large hotel in the Mombasa area, the Nyali Beach is set in lovely gardens and has excellent facilities including six restaurants, two swimming pools and free use of the adjacent Golf and Country Club.

✉ Nyali Beach ☎ 011-471567, fax 011-471987. Reservations through Block Hotels (➤ 101)

Diani Beach

Diani House (££) (HB)

A private guest-house offering four traditional double-bedroom *bandas* decorated in local style with lots of creative personal touches. Lovely seaside gardens, excellent food and very knowledgeable hosts (➤ 69), who can personally take guests snorkelling, big-game fishing, on local safari and on other excursions.

✉ PO Box 5002. Diani Beach road 1km south of main junction. ☎ fax 0127-2412. Bookings through Bush Homes (➤ 101)

Nomads (£–££)

A long-established Diani Beach favourite, Nomads offers very good value *bandas* (with en-suite bathrooms) and cottages in attractive grounds by the beach (➤ 93).

✉ PO Box 1, Ukunda. Diani Beach road (5km south of the main junction) ☎ 0127-2155, fax 0127-2391 ⓘ Closed May

Lamu Island

Peponi Hotel (£££)

Beautiful small-scale accommodation mixing modern luxury and simple local style to great effect. Very friendly hosts. Perfectly positioned on Shela Beach, though rather isolated for Lamu town (➤ 94).

✉ Shela Beach, PO Box 24 ☎ 0121-33154, fax 0121-33029

Petley's Inn (££)

This historic old waterfront house has long been infamous for its discomfort. Recent improvements, however, have transformed it into one of the nicest places to stay in Lamu, with lots of local touches. It is also as central as you can get and a great meeting place. Small swimming pool (➤ 94).

✉ Waterfront, next to ferry jetty ☎ 0121-33107

Yumbe House/Yumbe Villa (£)

A typical old Swahili stone house with cool patios full of tropical flowers and greenery, rooftop lounge areas and friendly staff. Rooms are basic but clean, with toilet, shower, mosquito nets and fans.

✉ PO Box 81, Lamu town ☎ 0121-33101, also fax

Malindi

The Driftwood Club (£–£££)
A favourite haunt of Anglo Kenyans and Malindi regulars, offering a wide range of accommodation from luxury private cottages to budget-class rooms (► 94). Swimming pool.
✉ PO Box 63, 3km south of town centre ☎ 0123-20155, fax 0123-30712

Fondo Wehu Guest House (£)
The best of Malindi's budget accommodations, in a central but quiet location, with friendly Anglo-Kenyan owners serving good breakfasts.
✉ PO Box 5367 ☎ 0123-30017

Sable Valley (££)
Located on the edge of the Shimba Hills National Park, this private guest house enjoys a stunning setting high on a hill with panoramic views over a beautiful unspoiled valley. Simple cottage accommodation, wonderful hosts; a perfect place to get away from it all. Swimming pool.
☎ Reservations/tariff through Bush Homes

Scorpio Villas (££) (HB)
Beautifully designed lush, quiet, small self-contained complex, a short walk away from the bustle of town. Great value. Swimming pool.
✉ PO Box 368, 1km south of town centre ☎ 0123-20194

Watamu

Hemingway's (£££)
Arguably the best hotel on the coast, Hemingways enjoys a magnificent situation (► 26) and belies the macho sporting swagger of its name by appealing to all visitors, irrespective of sporting predilections (► 114). Beautiful rooms, all with sea view. Superb food (► 95), free snorkelling trips, lovely swimming pools, attentive friendly staff.
✉ Turtle Bay ☎ 0122-32624, fax 0122-32256 🕐 Closed May, Jun

Private Homesteads
If you would like to stay on private homesteads in Kenya contact Bush Homes or Safari Consultants (below) who are agents for several such accommodations across the whole country. Many of these are colonial-style farms in very peaceful and beautiful settings, well off the beaten tourist track, owned by settlers whose Kenyan roots go back several decades. Don't expect five-star bedrooms; sleeping quarters can be modest, even basic. They are all equipped to provide a complete package of meals, guiding services and transport, and this is a marvellous way of seeing Kenya through the eyes of a local. If a tariff is not given in the listing for a private homestead this is because it is dependent upon exactly what the client wants and is subject to discussion.

Bush Homes of East Africa Ltd
✉ PO Box 56923, Nairobi ☎ 02-571647, fax 02-571665

Safari Consultants Ltd
✉ Orchard House, Upper Road, Little Cornard, Sudbury, Suffolk, England ☎ 0178- 228494, fax 01787-228096

Central Reservations
Block Hotels ☎ 02-540780, fax 02-540821; UK ☎ 0181 905 7383, fax 0181 905 6947.
Lonrho Hotels ☎ 02-216940, fax 02-216796; UK ☎ 0171 262 3409, fax 0171 262 7792; USA ☎ 813 387 0301, fax 813 387 0028.
Sarova Hotels ☎ 02-333233, fax 02-211472; UK 0171 589 6000, fax 0171 225 3476; USA 1-800 424 2862 or 212 986 8800, fax 212 986 1758.

Traditional Accommodation
Bandas are traditional chalet-style accommodation with *makuti* (palm-thatch) roofs. There may well be a gap between roof and walls to allow air circulation. This also allows bugs in and out, but you will be protected at night by a mosquito net. 'Knock-down' sprays are also usually provided. If not, ask.

Nairobi & Environs

Nairobi–Mombasa Train
Despite its 'Express' tag, this historic service (► 10) takes around 12 hours to cover 500km, stopping frequently at local stations. First-class accommodation is in two-berth cabins while second-class means sharing with three other people. Both first- and second-class fares are very reasonable and include bedding, breakfast and dinner. Book as early as possible, either direct with the station (see below) or through a local travel agent, as it is a very popular service.
☎ Nairobi station 02-221211
☎ Mombasa station 011-312221
First class 2,750 KSh; second class 1,930 KSh

Nairobi is still first base for most safari holidays, but the trend is to spend less time in the city (perhaps just the first night) or to move out to the suburbs. If you're travelling independently and arrive on the overnight flight you could head straight for Lake Naivasha (► 75).

City Centre
Ambassadeur (££)
Modestly priced, comfortable, international-class hotel. Very central but noisy, so ask for a double-glazed room. Good Indian restaurant on site. Guests can use the swimming pool of the New Stanley Hotel.
✉ Moi Avenue ☎ 02-336803. Reservations through Sarova Hotels (► 101)

New Stanley Hotel (££)
You can't get much more central than the New Stanley, right in the thick of the downtown action. A refit is about to breathe life back into this popular old place.
✉ Kimathi Street ☎ Reservations through Sarova Hotels (► 101)

Norfolk Hotel (£££)
Nairobi's most prestigious address for almost a century, the Norfolk is an institution. Rooms vary but most have every facility, and given that the city centre is a mere 5-minute walk away, the setting is surprisingly peaceful. Swimming pool.
✉ Harry Thuku Road, PO Box 58581 ☎ 02-335422. Reservations through Lonhro Hotels (► 101)

Serena (££)
It doesn't look anything special from the outside but inside it is one of the most popular haunts of Nairobi regulars. Lovely rooms.
✉ Nyerere Street ☎ 02-725111

Terminal (£)
Probably the most reliable and safe budget choice in the city centre. Friendly staff, comfortable clean rooms.
✉ Moktar Daddah Street ☎ 02-228817

Out of Town
Fairview (££)
A quiet country-style hotel set in large gardens, but only 5 minutes from the city centre by car. Good value.
✉ Bishops Road, PO Box 40842 ☎ 02-723211, fax 02-721320

Mayfair Court Hotel (£££)
A cheaper alternative to the Norfolk, 4km from the city centre, with comparable luxury, though less old-world style.
✉ Parklands Road, PO Box 74957 ☎ 02-746708

Safari Park Hotel (£££)
Arguably the best hotel in or near Nairobi (14km from the centre), set in 26 beautiful hectares with superb swimming pools and many other sports facilities. All rooms have four-poster beds.
✉ Thika Road, PO Box 45038 ☎ 02-802493, fax 02-802477

Windsor Golf and Country Club (£££)
Set in glorious grounds of around 80 hectares this recently built resort complex offers spacious Victorian-style guest accommodation with every luxury.
✉ Kigwa Road, 15km north of city centre ☎ 02-862300, fax 02-802322

Central Highlands

This region is famous for its colonial hotels and its two prestigious treetop lodges. The latter are specially designed accommodations on stilts, built beside a salt-lick (a naturally occuring deposit of salt) or a water-hole, for the purpose of sedentary game viewing. Large picture windows, balconies and walkways give grandstand views while bunker hides offer covert observation.

Aberdare Country Club and The Ark (£££)
The Country Club accommodation is in roomy chalets, several of which are ranged up a steep hill which offers superb views over the Aberdare Range. Service is immaculate and food is excellent. Swimming pool. Access to the Ark is only possible from here (► 63, 99).
✆ Reservations for the Aberdare Country Club and the Ark through Lonrho Hotels (► 101)

Blue Posts Hotel (££)
A famous old colonial hotel, established in 1908, recently refurbished to a high standard, with lovely gardens which offer a glimpse of the Chania Falls.
✉ Nairobi-Muranga'a Road, Thika ✆ 0151-22241

The Kentmere Club (££)
A little bit of old England, complete with an authentic re-creation of an English country pub. Accommodation is in wooden cottages set in beautiful gardens. Very good value (► 99).
✉ Old Limuru road ✆ 0154-41053-42053

Mount Kenya Safari Club (£££)
Probably the most famous hotel name in Kenya (► 65, 99). All the rooms are superb, but the chalets by the river are particularly romantic. Lovely swimming pool. Golf, horse-riding, tennis courts and bowling green.
✉ Near Nanyuki ✆ 0176-22960. Reservations through Lonrho Hotels (► 101)

Outspan Hotel and Treetops (£££)
The Outspan is a charming old colonial hotel with spacious rooms and all the trimmings; lovely gardens, fine views of Mount Kenya, swimming pool, golf course, snooker table, log fires etc (► 67, 99). Lord Baden-Powell, founder of the Boy Scouts, lived the last years of his life here from 1938 until his death in 1941. The Outspan takes its name from the South African verb 'to outspan', meaning to unyoke (animals) and recalls the colonial period when Kenyan settlers used to unyoke their ox-wagon trains and rest here.
Access to Treetops is only possible from here.
✉ Near Nyeri ✆ 0171-2424. Reservations through Block Hotels (► 101)

White Rhino Hotel (££)
A long-established colonial-style hotel, slightly fraying at the edges, but still atmospheric, with pleasant gardens; a much cheaper alternative than the Outspan (see above).
✉ Corner of Mumba Road and Kenyatta Road, Nyeri ✆ 0171-30934

Night Viewing
As most activity occurs by night at the treetop lodges, powerful floodlights are used to illuminate the animals, and guests who have retired for the night can choose to be alerted by buzzers in their rooms when nocturnal visitors arrive. Some lodges provide a grading system to help decide whether or not it's worth climbing out of bed; for example, two buzzes may indicate elephant or rhino while three buzzes signals the arrival of big cats.

Rift Valley & Western Kenya

A Flying Visit
In the romantic days of flying boats, between 1937 and 1950, Lake Naivasha was a staging post between London and Cape Town with travellers staying a night at Lake Naivasha Country Club (then known as the Lake Hotel).

Rift Valley

Lake Baringo
Lake Baringo Club (££) (FB)
The place for bird-watchers (➤ 73). Accommodation is in simple *bandas*. Good value.
☎ **Reservations through Block Hotels (➤ 101)**

Lake Naivasha
Crater Lake Camp (£££) (FB)
A beautiful tented camp crafted entirely from local materials and fitting in perfectly with its 'hidden world' setting (➤ 72). Each tent has a four-poster bed, en-suite bathroom and a glorious view of the lake.
✉ **Crater Lake Sanctuary, Lake Naivasha** ☎ **Via Mythos Ltd 333-569 224826**

Elsamere Conservation Centre (£) (FB)
Here in the grounds of Joy Adamson's former home are simply furnished cottages, each facing Lake Naivasha (➤ 75). Popular with wild-life researchers and conservationists.
✉ **Lake Naivasha** ☎ **0311-21055, fax 0311-21074**
❓ **No children under 8**

Lake Naivasha Country Club (£££)
Set in lovely gardens, this is the most luxurious hotel on the lake, with a long colonial history. Swimming pool.
✉ **PO Box 15, Lake Naivasha** ☎ **0311-20013. Reservations through Block Hotel (➤ 101)**

Ololerai Farm (£–££)
The Barton's Farm (as it is also known to distinguish it from another Ololerai residence on the lake), enjoys a paradisaical setting right on the Naivasha shoreline and John and Barbara Barton are wonderful hosts. The farm itself attracts various wildlife. Accommodation is in simply furnished chalets.
☎ **0311-21067. Reservations/tariff through Safari Consultants (➤ 101)**

Lake Nakuru
(➤ 105, Game Park Lodges)

Western Kenya

Kericho
Tea Hotel (££)
Situated in the lush greenery of Kenya's tea belt, this is the best-known hotel in Western Kenya with the atmosphere and facilities of a country club. Rooms with views over the tea plantations; cottages are also available.
✉ **PO Box 75, Moi Highway** ☎ **0361-30004, fax 0361-20576**

Kitale
Lokitela Farm (££)
This working farm is an attraction in its own right and is particularly good for ornithologists, with 260 species of birds recorded in the gardens and adjacent forest. Host Tony Mills is a very experienced safari guide (both bird-watching and big game). Ideal base for Mount Elgon. Accommodation is in simply furnished chalets.
☎ **Reservations/tariff through Bush Homes (➤ 101)**

Nyahururu
Thomson's Falls Lodge (£)
Stay in the original brick cottages built by the English settlers in the 1930s or in the newer Swiss-chalet style buildings. (➤ 79, 99).
✉ **PO Box 38, Nyahururu** ☎ **0365-22006, fax 0365-32170**

Game Park Lodges

Amboseli
Ol Tukai (£££)
Beautifully decorated chalets, each with a view of Kilimanjaro and a splendid swimming pool.
☎ **Reservations through Block Hotels (➤ 101)**

Lake Nakuru
Sarova Lion Hill Lodge (£££)
Occupies a fine elevated position set back from the lake. Simply decorated chalets; nice atmosphere. Swimming pool.
☎ **Reservations through Sarova Hotels (➤ 101)**

Lewa Downs
Wilderness Trails (£££)
One of Kenya's original ranches. Accommodation is either in the ranch house or cottages (➤ 65).
☎ **Reservations through Bush Homes (➤ 101)**

Masai Mara
Governors' Camp/Little Governors' Camp (£££)
Occupying prime sites on and near the Mara River respectively, Governors' and Little Governors' are two of Africa's original luxury tented camps with every comfort. Food and service is exemplary.
☎ **Reservations 02-331871, fax 02-726427**

Samburu
Samburu Game Lodge (£££)
The original and still the best lodge in Samburu with a wonderful position and tastefully decorated rooms, all facing the river. Swimming pool.
☎ **Reservations through Block Hotels (➤ 101)**

Shaba
Sarova Shaba Lodge (£££)
A Robinson Crusoe fantasy of palm-thatched houses on stilts set in glorious grounds. Rooms very tastefully appointed in local style. Swimming pool.
☎ **Reservations through Sarova Hotels (➤ 101)**

Shimba Hills
Shimba Lodge (£££)
A charming treehouse lodge (➤ 47). No children.
☎ **Reservations through Block Hotels (➤ 100)** ❓ **Sable Valley (➤ 101), a private guest house, is also within the Shimba Hills**

Taita Hills
Salt Lick Hilton Safari Lodge (£££)
Excellent game viewing in the dry season from Kenya's most bizarre treetops-style hotel (➤ 47). Swimming pool and other facilities at nearby Hilton Safari Lodge.
☎ **147-30250, fax 147-30235**
☎ **Reservations 02-334000; UK 0345 581595; USA 1-800 445 8667**

Tsavo East
Voi Safari Lodge £££
Set on a clifftop overlooking a watering hole, occupying what is probably the most dramatic position of any accommodation in Kenya.
☎ **Reservations African Tours and Hotels 02-336858, fax 02-218109**

Tsavo West
Kilaguni Lodge £££
An old favourite, but ageing well. Excellent waterhole position (abundant with game) and wonderful views.
☎ **Reservations African Tours and Hotels 02-336858, fax 02-218109**

Tented Camps
Tented camps are a far cry from roughing it. The tents are generally the size of small marquees, big enough to accommodate two beds and a rear area, which is divided by a flap to become the bathroom, and usually features all mod cons (however, there is generally no electricity). None the less, the vast majority of guests find the experience immensely enjoyable and very atmospheric, particularly at night, when a camp fire is lit and soft glowing gas lamps are the only form of illumination.

Tariffs
Game park lodges and camps tariffs vary considerably. Check what meals are included in the price (it's normal to include dinner but lunch may be extra). Some lodges include game drives in the price of accommodation, others don't. To avoid an unpleasant surprise check in advance.

Arts & Crafts

Opening Times
Shop hours are normally from Monday to Saturday 8:30 to 5:30, though some shops close for lunch and on Saturday afternoon. Markets are open Monday to Saturday from around 8 to early afternoon.

Curio and Craft Shops
'Curio shops' range from street stalls to the African Heritage Centre superstore, all selling handicrafts and perhaps genuine antiques, though you should always be sceptical of any claims made. Many of the establishments listed are self-help community projects or have charitable status. Prices in such places are generally fixed, unless you are buying in quantity.

Fabrics
The most popular item is the *kanga*, a simple rectangle of colourful cloth, printed with bright designs and often featuring an acerbic Swahili proverb. A *kikoi* is a similar length of cloth for men, usually thicker and often striped. The coast is famed for its fabrics and the place to go is Biashara Street, Mombasa, where the latest fashions are on display even before they hit Nairobi. Look, too, for batiks and wax paintings which make lovely wall hangings.

Soapstone
Kenya's most distinctive souvenir medium, soapstone, is quarried from Western Kenya and comes in delicate shades of pink and white. Some of the carvings, particularly of people are very beautiful, very sensuous and very reasonably priced. There is such a large choice that it's worth hunting about to find the best.

Masks and Tribal Regalia
Although masks are often the most striking of all the goods on offer, they are also the least likely to be of Kenyan origin, imported from other parts of the continent, mostly West Africa. Shields, spears, headdresses, drums and beads are more likely to be mass-produced than genuine Masai produced. Let the price be your guide.

Woodcarvings
Woodcarvings come in every shape and size and are an excellent buy. *Makonde* woodcarving is a Tanzanian tradition using ebony – not illegal, but ecologically unsound. However, most *makonde* in Kenya's curio shops is actually fake, light wood blackened by shoe polish. If pressed, and if he thinks it is to his advantage, the seller may even admit this, but the weight of the wood (ebony is very heavy) is the most reliable indicator.

Art in Lamu
Lamu is famous for a different type of wood-working; Zanzibar-style wooden chests, coffee tables and beds. Look into any one of the many small workshops along the main street. You'll also see a good number of model dhows. Sadly most of these are often less than portable, but just looking is fun and there is much less hassle here than on the mainland.

Aladdin's Caves
Many of the emporia of Ndia Kuu (Main Street) are like miniature Aladdin's Caves with furnishings, *kilims*, silver tribal jewellery and gleaming lamps straight out of the Arabian Nights. There's quite a hard sell.

Markets & Shops

Markets

The Coast

Mombasa

Mackinnon Market

Very colourful with the best of the coast's fruits, including exotic varieties that you won't see in your hotel, such as jackfruit and soursop.

✉ **Digo Road**

Floating Market

A number of craft stalls formed by a local co-operative are moored in Tudor Creek and provide a great photo opportunity as well as a shopping trip. It's not a real market, but it's enjoyable none the less, and with no hassle.

☎ **011-472213, Jahazi Marine Ltd for dhow trips to the floating market, or speak to your hotel tour representative**

Lamu

Lamu Market

This is the most colourful daily gathering in Lamu and takes place every morning with a fairly sparse selection of fruits and vegetables.

✉ **Harambee Road, by the fort**

Malindi

Crafts Market

Expensive and lots of hassle!

✉ **Harambee Road, by the old town**

Nairobi

City Market

The most famous and colourful of Nairobi's markets. Food and flower stalls plus crafts.

✉ **Muindi Mbingu Street**

Kariakor

A real craftsman's market with basketware the speciality. Look out, too, for sandals made from old tyres.

✉ **Between Racecourse Road and Ring Road**

Masai Market

Jewellery, baskets, gourds, *kangas* etc, at a fraction of prices asked elsewhere and with minimum hassle.

✉ **Next to roundabout between Murang'a Road and Kijabe Street** 🕐 **Tue 9–3**

Western Kenya

Kisumu

Kisumu Market

The biggest and best in the west for atmosphere, colour and hustle and bustle. Fruit and vegetables, household goods, and not a tourist in sight!

✉ **Moi Avenue**

Shops

The Coast

Mombasa and Environs

African Heritage Centre See Nairobi entry (▶ 108).

✉ **Serena Beach Hotel, Shanzu Beach, north of Mombasa** ☎ **011-485721**

Akamba Woodcarvers

Woodcarvings, sculptures and other decorative goods. Popular with tour operators.

✉ **Port Reitz Road, near the airport** ☎ **011-432241**

Bombolulu Workshops

A tourist attraction in its own right, turning out a wide range of excellent quality goods at reasonable prices (▶ 37), particularly strong on women's fashion.

✉ **Malindi Road, Bombolulu, 3km north of Mombasa** ☎ **011-471704**

Shopping Strategy

Before you buy anything look in one of the quality fixed-price shops where you will be left to browse in peace. This will give you an idea of what is available and the approximate price range. Only then should you try out your haggling skills at the markets and roadside curio stalls. Be prepared for a mixture of good-natured banter, never-take-no-for-an-answer persistence, hard-luck stories (sadly often true) and downright lies about the quality and provenance of goods. You'll either love it or hate it! But, if it all gets too much you can always go back to the fixed-price shops.

Beware of pickpockets in crowded markets, always check your change and double-check your bill when you buy several items.

Books

Out of Africa by Karen Blixen (➤ 14) is a beautiful if rather slow and rambling evocation of colonial days. For a very different, pacier style of romp set around the same period, pick up *White Mischief* by James Fox. A grim and gritty portrait of modern-day Nairobi is painted in *Going Down River Road* by Meja Mwangi. Look out, too, for the many beautiful and often remarkable coffee-table books illustrating the people, wildlife and landscapes of Kenya.

Jahazi Trading Co

Reputable, though rather expensive, traders in *kilims*, antique furniture, old silver tribal jewellery and other eastern goods.

✉ **Ndia Kuu, Old Town, Mombasa** ☎ **0127-51234**

Labeka

High quality carvings, antiques and jewellery but at sensible prices. Try Harria's Gift Shop, also on Moi Avenue.

✉ **Moi Avenue** ☎ **011-312232**

Lamu
Gypsies

By far the classiest shop in Lamu, selling furniture and a small range of jewellery (they also have details of houses and villas for rent).

✉ **Harambee Street (next to Rumours at Baraka Coffee Shop**

Malindi
Woodcarving Co-operative

Good quality items direct from the craftsmen.

✉ **Old town** ☎ **No tel**

Nairobi and Environs
African Heritage Centre

This should be the first stop for any serious shopper, offering the best of Kenyan and other African crafts. The Libra House superstore, a few kilometres out of town, has even more choice, with minibuses shuttling from Kenyatta Avenue four times a day.

✉ **City Centre branch, Kenyatta Avenue** ☎ **02-333157** ✉ **Libra House, Mombasa Road** ☎ **02-554547** ❓ **Libra House is 7km from the city centre**

Colpro

If you want genuine safari clothing this is one of the city's best shops.

✉ **Kimathi Street** ☎ **02-224430**

The Glass Gallery

If money is no object this is the place; African images etched on goblets, vases, mirrors etc, plus stained glassware.

✉ **Lonrho House, Kaunda Street**

Kazuri Bead Centre

Over a hundred women work at this beads, jewellery and pottery factory, turning out some beautiful items (also in African Heritage Centre). Visits include a tour of the workshops as well as a superb range of beads on sale in the factory.

✉ **Mbagathi Ridge, Karen** ☎ **02-882362** 🕐 **Mon–Sat 8:30–4:30, Sun (shop only) 11–4:30** 🔄 **Karen Blixen Museum (➤ 59)**

Kichaka

Kenya's best selection of crafts, particularly good for hand-dyed and hand-stencilled clothing, from caftans to T-shirts.

✉ **Kijabe Street** ☎ **02-228807**

Kumbu Kumbu

Wood carvings from some of East Africa's finest artists.

✉ **Nairobi Hilton Arcade, Mama Ngina Street** ☎ **02-222074**

Lenana Forest Centre

A fascinating gemstone and mineral workshop where you can watch stones being cut and polished before you buy.

✉ **256 Collins Road, Karen** ☎ **02-882297**

Museum Hill Centre

Close to the National Museum, this is a small mall with a Kenya Wildlife Service shop which sells trinkets and various ethnic odds and ends at very reasonable prices (the shop attached to the museum is also worth a look, though its prices are not so keen).

✉ **Museum Road**

The Nation (Westland Sundries) Bookshop

Excellent range of books on all aspects of Kenya, including many beautiful, superbly illustrated 'coffee-table' tomes.

✉ **Kimathi Street, next to the New Stanley Hotel** ☎ 02-333507

Ostrich Park Arts and Crafts Village

There are ostriches on show here, but the Arts and Crafts Village is the real attraction, making and selling a wide range of high-quality souvenirs and numerous gift items.

✉ **Off Langata Road, Karen**
🕐 **Daily 9–5:30** 🚌 **Giraffe Centre (▶ 58)** 💷 **Small entrance fee**

Siafu

Baffled what to buy for children? Look here for a better class of wooden carved animals, jigsaws and all sorts of clever animal-themed toys.

✉ **Karen, next to the Horseman Restaurant**

The Spinner's Web

Natural fabrics, woven goods and some jewellery.

✉ **Longonot Place, Kijabe Street (behind Norfolk Hotel)** ☎ 02-228647

Tropical Crafts

Soft furnishings and fabric specialists in *kangas, kikoyis, kitenges* and rugs, as well as wood carving.

✉ **Muindi Mbingu Street (opposite City Market)** ☎ 02-224005

Utamaduni Crafts Centre

Around 18 units under one roof selling a comprehensive range of goods, but at inflated prices. Dance displays every afternoon.

✉ **Langata Road, Karen**
🕐 **Daily 10–6** 🚌 **Giraffe Centre (▶ 58)**

Zanzibar Curio Shop

Good, all-purpose souvenirs and crafts shop which has been going strong since 1936; batik, jewellery, safari wear, Arab chests, sisal baskets, ebony carvings, wood carvings, soapstone carvings, brass and copperware, African semi-precious stones.

✉ **Moi Avenue, next to Nairobi Sports House** ☎ 02-222704

Rest of Kenya

Nanyuki
Mount Kenya Safari Club

Beautiful craft and art gallery shop with a few affordable items in between the expensive works of art and genuine antiques. Very browsable (▶ 65).

✉ **PO Box 35, Nanyuki**
☎ **0176-22960**

Spinners' and Weavers' Co-operative

Rugs, jumpers, shawls and other articles produced at the wheel and on hand looms at reasonable prices.

✉ **1km north of town, on C76 (Nyahururu Road)**

Music

Pacy percussion, jangly guitars and infectious rhythms are the hallmark of modern Kenyan music which has been strongly influenced by bands from Zaire and Tanzania. One of the most popular bands in Kenya is Les Wanyika (from Tanzania) and anything by them is worth a listen.

Don't buy cheap pirate cassettes from itinerant vendors (unless you get a chance to listen first) as the quality is often appalling. Large hotels often stock a limited range of bona fide cassettes but the best selection is to be found in Nairobi or Mombasa where you'll find cassettes, CD and vinyl.

Children's Attractions

Catering for Children
Hotels generally make few provisions for children so a good-sized, child-friendly swimming pool may be essential to your sanity. Organise a travel diary or some kind of pictorial tick list of all the animals and birds you see (there are many good field guides which you can use). It will help concentration and give them wonderful memories to take home.

Natural Attractions
Kenya is mainly for adults; it has no theme parks, no interactive museums, no water parks; in fact barely a single attraction designed for children. On the plus side it has marvellous beaches and animals aplenty.

Nairobi and Environs
Bomas of Kenya
Younger children will probably enjoy exploring inside the tribal thatched huts and around the homesteads, while older ones may enjoy the tribal dancing too, though it is overlong, even for adults (➤ 58).

Carnivore Restaurant
Saturday afternoon activities for kids include acrobats, puppet shows and face painting (➤ 98).

Giraffe Centre (Langata)
This giraffe-feeding station (➤ 58) is without doubt the most child-friendly attraction in the country (adults love it too). Ask in advance if you can join a children's school party in the morning and also to see their educational video on wildlife conservation.

Nairobi Animal Orphanage
Funded by Dutch schoolchildren there is a good variety of animals in this zoo-like compound. With older children you could combine this with a trip to the adjacent Nairobi National Park.
🖂 **Langata Road, beside main gate of Nairobi National Park**
☎ **02-501081** 🚶 **Moderate**

Ostrich Park
Populated by birds of all ages, from tiny balls of fluff to the tallest on earth. While the kids feed them titbits, Mum or Dad can do a spot of serious shopping (➤ 109).
🖂 **Off Langata Road, Karen**
☎ **02-891051** ⏰ **Daily 9–6**
🚶 **Cheap**

Utamaduni Crafts Centre
Visit the Giraffe Centre at Langata then come here for your shopping. There is a children's play area, a toyshop and dance displays every afternoon.
🖂 **Off Langata Road, Karen**

The Coast

North of Mombasa
Bamburi Nature Trail
If you're staying north of Mombasa then Bamburi is an excellent alternative to a national game park, and very much cheaper (➤ 36). Here sightings of some of Africa's larger animals (hippos, crocodiles and antelopes) in near-natural conditions are guaranteed all within a few minutes' walk of each other.

Bombolulu
Like the Bomas of Kenya (➤ 58), there are tribal thatched homesteads and exotic dancing. However, at Bombolulu the quality is higher, the dancing is shorter, the shopping is excellent, and all proceeds go to a good cause (➤ 37).

Gedi Ruins
Older more intrepid children may enjoy scrambling about the ruins, particularly if you tell them about Gedi's haunted reputation (➤ 36 – look out for bag-snatching monkeys!) This can also be combined with a trip to

Watamu (see Malindi and Watamu Marine Park – ➤ 26, 42).

Kenya Marineland
The dhow trip which comes here may take too long (and is expensive), but if you make your own way most kids will enjoy seeing sharks, rays, crocodiles and other creatures (➤ 39).

Malindi and Watamu Marine Park
If children are of snorkelling age then they'll be agog at the spectacle beneath the waves. Whether you enter the park from Malindi or Watamu, both require only a short boat ride and depart from a good beach; Turtle Bay at Watamu is magnificent, and perfect for children. Hire a canoe from Hemingway's or Ocean Sports and explore the tiny little islands close to the shore (➤ 26, 42).

Mamba Crocodile Village
If your children want to see crocodiles, this is the place, as there are thousands of them! The small ones are an amazing sight (➤ 44).

Pirates Beach Bar and Restaurant
Mum and Dad can have a drink at the bar while the kids amuse themselves on the water slides here. There's only two slides (one fast, one gentle) so its hardly an aquapark, but it's very popular none the less. There's live music at the restaurant at weekends.
📧 **Kenyatta Municipal Beach**
☎ **011-486441** 🕐 **Daily**
🎞 **20 slides for 200 KSh; unlimited slides for 300 Ksh**

On Safari
It is a waste of time and money taking younger children on safari. They get bored by the long hours of driving and will probably not appreciate wildlife sightings at 100m distance. Wait until they are at least 10 years old and have expressed an interest in wildlife.

The Ark/Treetops
Children under 7 are generally not allowed here (nor in any of the other treetop lodges), but enquire about special children's nights. Staying up late and seeing elephants close up could be a very special treat (➤ 62, 67)

Masai Mara
On the whole children are not to going to enjoy long game drives, so if you must take them on safari, bring them here, where sightings are almost guaranteed and you can drive right up to lions (➤ 20). The next best choice for plenty of game in a confined area is Amboseli (➤ 17).

Mount Kenya Animal Orphanage
The second most charming place for children in Kenya (after the Giraffe Centre). In many cases children can touch the animals, and they may well be allowed to feed them too (➤ 65, Mount Kenya Safari Club).

Tribal Dancing
Many hotels put on displays of tribal dancing, often involving Samburu and Masai warriors. This is usually a colourful spectacle which will appeal to most younger children.

Beware
Beware of the African sun; keep children covered at night and protected against insect bites; warn them not to feed monkeys (or indeed any wild animals) which can become very nasty and bite.

Nightlife/Dhow Trips

Clubbing It
Most clubs are open quite early, around 8 or 9PM weekdays, slightly later at weekends, though things don't usually get going until around midnight. Admission charges are low (around 100 KSh) and unless you are in a tourist trap (eg the International Casino complex) drinks are cheap. Look in the Friday edition of *The Daily Nation* for what's on.

Many nightclubs are simply pick-up joints for prostitutes, the most infamous name on the tourist/ex-pat circuit being the New Florida, both in Nairobi and in Mombasa. The clubs listed below are rather more respectable, but men alone should still be very wary of over-eager local females.

Nightlife

North of Mombasa

Diani Beach
Diani Casino
Part of the International Casino chain offering Black Jack, American Roulette, , Let it Ride (➤ International Casino, Nairobi, 113) and slot machines.
✉ **Diani Reef Grand Hotel, Diani Beach** ☎ **0127-2159** 🕐 **Daily**

Forty Thieves Beach Bar
Open-air disco by the beach.
✉ **Diani Beach, 3km from the main junction** 🕐 **Wed, Fri, Sat**

Malindi
Casino Malindi
✉ **Lamu Road, Malindi** ☎ **0123-21104** 🕐 **Daily**

Stardust Disco
The biggest and probably the best club in Malindi.
✉ **Lamu Road, Malindi** ☎ **0123-20338** 🕐 **Tel for opening days**

Nyali
Bora Bora
Probably the best disco on this stretch of coast and conveniently close to several major hotels.
✉ **Mombasa–Malindi Road (just south of Whitesands, Travellers Beach and Bamburi Beach hotels)** ☎ **011-485076**

Nyali Casino
Part of the International Casino chain offering Black Jack, American Roulette, Let it Ride (➤ International Casino, Nairobi, 113) and slot machines.
✉ **Nyali Beach Hotel, Nyali** ☎ **011-471551** 🕐 **Daily**

Nairobi
Bubbles
Contemporary dance music for a young crowd. Occasional live music (sometimes the popular Pressmen – ➤ Hard Rock Café below).
✉ **International Casino complex, Museum Hill** ☎ **02-742600** 🕐 **Daily**

Cantina Club
Locals' club with *nyama choma* (➤ 80) and an excellent alternative to the Carnivore/Simba Saloon (➤ 113) if you want to 'go native'. Slightly older crowd, so usually a good mellow atmosphere.
✉ **Wilson Airport Road, Langata** ☎ **02-506085** 🕐 **Daily**

Galileo's Members Club
Dancing, dinner, live music, cabaret and great views of Nairobi by night.
✉ **International Casino complex, Museum Hill** ☎ **02-742600** 🕐 **Closed Mon**

Hard Rock Café
You will know what to expect from the food and décor, but it's the Pressmen (a well-established Nairobi pop-and-rock band) who make the visit really worth while.
✉ **Mezzanine 2, Barclays Plaza** ☎ **02-220802** 🕐 **Pressmen usually play Wed, Fri, Sat (☎ to confirm)**

International Casino
Black Jack, American Roulette, Pontoon, 'Let it Ride' (a game in which it is claimed a player can win up to 75,000 KSh in the first hand) and slot machines are the gambling attractions here. There are also several restaurants and nightclubs.
✉ **Museum Hill** ☎ **02-742600**
🕐 **Daily**

L'Ora Blu
Nairobi's latest nightclub is aimed at the more affluent end of the market and is appealing to businessmen and well-heeled visitors. It features live entertainment and an à la carte restaurant.
✉ **Corner House, opposite Hilton Hotel** ☎ **02-223662**
🕐 **Daily 5PM–5AM**

Simba Saloon
Part of the famous Carnivore (► 98) and a great place to dance off an excess of food in the open air. Touristy but well patronised by the locals, with a good fusion of African and Western music, both live and recorded. Themes change nightly (Jazz, African, Soul etc) so check what's on or see *The Daily Nation*.
✉ **Carnivore Restaurant, Langata Road** ☎ **02-501775**
🕐 **Closed Mon, Tue**

Zanze Bar
A well-established trendy and popular club featuring soul, karaoke and funk nights, plus live jazz on Sunday afternoons.
✉ **Kenya Cinema Plaza, Moi Avenue** ☎ **02-222568** 🕐 **Closed Mon**

Zig-Zag
Possibly the best locals' club in Nairobi with great music

on two dance floors, including not only the usual reggae and mainstream sounds but excellent African music. Cheap beer, terrific atmosphere, great dancing and (so far) hassle-free. For details of special nights see *The Daily Nation*.
✉ **New Hurlingham Plaza, Argwings Kodhek Road**

Dhow Trips

North of Mombasa

Fort Jesus/Mombasa by Night
A romantic cruise along the floodlit waterfront of Mombasa old town landing at historic Fort Jesus (► 34) where you are met by period-dressed Arab and Portuguese 'guards' bearing fire torches. A sound-and-light show illustrates the turbulent history of the fort, before a lobster or steak dinner is enjoyed al fresco. There is an optional extension to the Bora Bora nightclub for the midnight cabaret, then to Nyali Casino.
☎ **011-472213 to book**

Kenya Marineland Dhow
An evening visit to Kenya Marineland (► 39) with an African meal at a beautiful creekside restaurant, and entertainment on board.
☎ **011-485248 to book**

Tamarind Dhow
Two trips daily, for lunch and dinner. The latter is very romantic, sailing along the floodlit waterfront of Mombasa old town, with a gourmet lobster (or steak) dinner, and dancing to a live band (► 92).
☎ **011-471948 to book**

Dhow Cruising
Dhows are traditional Arab sailing boats which have plied the East African coast for over a thousand years, their design virtually unchanged. Built entirely from wood, they were used to transport such romantic cargoes as spices, wooden chests and carpets between India and East Africa, and always set sail in the times of the monsoon winds.

Sport

The Water Sporting Season
Activities on or under the water are curtailed during the Kenyan winter. Big-game fishing is generally put on hold between June and July. Diving and snorkelling cease from May to August.

Watersports

North of Mombasa

Lamu
Peponi Hotel
Diving, snorkelling, windsurfing tuition, waterskiing.
✉ Shela Beach ☎ 0121-33421

Malindi
Driftwood Club
Big-game fishing and diving.
✉ 2km south of Malindi town centre, on the Mombasa road
☎ 0123-20155.

Watamu
Hemingway's
An internationally renowned centre of excellence for big-game fishing, particularly sailfish and marlin. Tag and release is encouraged to conserve stocks and help monitor fish movements.
✉ Turtle Bay, Watamu
☎ 0122-32624

Ocean Sports
A very good reputation for big-game fishing and diving.
✉ Turtle Bay, Watamu
☎ 0122-32008

South of Mombasa

Diani Beach
Nomad's/Diani Diving
Big-game fishing, windsurfing and diving.
✉ Diani Beach ☎ 0127-2142
🕐 Closed May

Shimoni
Pemba Channel Fishing Club
The Pemba Channel is famous for big-game fishing, with huge marlin and tiger sharks commonplace.
☎ PO Box 86952, Mombasa
☎ 011-313749 🕐 Closed late

March/early April until early August

Rift Valley
Windsurfing and waterskiing are possible on Lake Baringo (contact the Lake Baringo Club ► 104) but beware crocodiles!

Freshwater Fishing
Nile perch abounds in Lake Victoria with frequent catches of over 500kg. There are two exclusive fishing clubs on neighbouring islands to choose from. Both are served by twice-daily flights from the Masai Mara.

Mfangano Island Camp
A romantic camp with accommodation in clay and thatch *bandas* in local style.
☎ 02-331871 (Governors' Camps)

Rusinga Island
Beautiful lodge with accommodation for up to eight guests in thatched lakeside *bandas*.
✉ Lake Victoria ☎ Lonrho Hotels (► 101)

White-water Rafting

Savage Wilderness Safaris
Raft along the Tana River just north of Tsavo East park or along the Athi River, which runs through Tsavo East (no previous experience needed, minimum age 14). Enquire, too, about sea kayaking on the coast and on the Rift Valley lakes. One-day trips along the Tana River depart from Nairobi at 8AM and return around 5:30PM.
☎ 02-521590

Golf

Nairobi and Environs
Windsor Golf and Country Club
Claimed to be the best championship golf course in Africa and recommended by the PGA of Europe. Also features a large heated outdoor swimming pool and fishing and horse riding opportunities.

✉ Kigwa Road, 15km north of Nairobi ☎ 02-862300

Coast
Diani Golf Club
New and still rather raw but shaping up nicely – the best course on the south coast.

✉ Diani Beach Road
☎ 0127-2620

Nyali Golf & Country Club
The best course on the north coast. Squash and tennis courts and a swimming pool also on site.

✉ Links Road, Nyali ☎ 011-472632

Ballooning
The most romantic place for a balloon trip in Kenya is over the Masai Mara. On touchdown you will enjoy a full 'English breakfast' with champagne in the bush, before being taken on a game drive, then back to camp. Mara Balloon Safaris are one of the oldest and most competent operators and fly right over the River Mara.

✉ Mara Balloon Safaris, Governor's Camp, Masai Mara
☎ 02–331871

Microlight Flying
A great thrill (though not for the faint-hearted), and at around £35 per quarter hour, a fraction of the price of a balloon ride. Enquire at Nomad's on Diani Beach (☎ 0127-2155) for coast flights and with Adventures Aloft for Masai Mara flights (☎ 02-221439).

Horse-racing

Nairobi Racecourse
This beautiful little racecourse is a great favourite with ex-pats, better-off locals and visitors in the know.

✉ Ngong Road, 10km southwest of city centre ☎ 02-566108 🕐 Most Sun; closed Aug, Sep. Look in *The Sunday Nation*

Horse Riding
Horse riding in Kenya is a great thrill as you can approach (non-predatory) animals much closer on horseback than you can in a vehicle or on foot. Try the following, all of which offer lessons for inexperienced riders:

**Aberdare Country Club (► 63);
Kitengela Polo Club, Karen
☎ 02-882782;
Lewa Downs (► 65);
Mount Kenya Safari Club (► 65)**

Experienced riders may like to consider:
**Simply Natural (☎ 02-217028 – Nairobi office; ☎ 011-313868 – Mombasa office)
Offbeat Safaris 16-day safaris through Masailand and the Loitas Hills
Also riding in the Rift Valley
☎ Contact via Safari Consultants in the UK, 01787 228494**

For a less stenuous canter along the beach north of Mombasa, enquire at Mamba Village (► 44).

Disclaimer
Note that you will probably have to sign a disclaimer before engaging in some of these activities and that your personal insurance may not cover you in the event of accident.

What's On When

Other Events

January *International Billfishing Tournament*, Malindi
February *Mombasa Fishing Festival*
March *Kenya Open Golf Championship*
November *Malindi Fishing Festival*

There are only a few annual events in the Kenyan calendar that are of interest to visitors.

Agricultural Shows

If you're from farming stock yourself you may enjoy one of these rural jamborees which are based on the British style of farm show and are organised by the Agricultural Society of Kenya (ASK). However, even for non-farming Westerners, they are generally colourful occasions. The Mombasa Show takes place the first week in August; the Nairobi Show the first week in October. There are many more shows held all over the country. Ask around and look in *The Nation* for details.

The Safari Rally

If you have any experience of driving in Kenya you'll understand why this is classified as one of the world's toughest motor rallies. The route circles much of Kenya on its 4,000km, four-day course, so there's a chance it will be near where you are staying. It is held over the Easter weekend. See *The Daily Nation* for details.
☎ 02-720382 (AA Nairobi HQ)

The Rhino Charge

Motorsports fans should also note that there is another well-publicised rally event on the first weekend in June. The Rhino Charge raises money for rhino conservation with participants donating huge sums (minimum of 750,000 KSh) for the pleasure of driving suicidally from point A to point B in as little time as possible. The

start and finish locations are a closely guarded secret, released just before the race. See *The Nation* or listen to the radio.
☎ 02-720382 (AA Nairobi HQ)

The Great Wildebeest Migration

Between early July and September each year the Masai Mara is home to one of the natural world's greatest spectacles. The great wildebeest migration involves some 2 million wildebeest (gnu) and around half a million zebras (accompanied by many thousands of gazelle), trekking north from the adjoining Serengeti National Park in Tanzania, in search of fresh grazing. Following on, also in search of fresh food, are lions, leopards, cheetahs, hyenas and vultures. The crossing of the River Mara, which is running at full flood at this time of year, is the wildebeest's greatest test, and is the subject of endless numbers of photographs. Many falter and are swept away to drown or end up in the jaws of hungry crocodiles. The vast majority survive, and return the following year.

Ramadan

The main consequence of the Islamic month of fasting on the tourist is that the occasional restaurant is closed for lunch. However, if you are on the coast at the end of the period you may see the celebration of *Id ul Fitr. Maulidi*, the prophet's birthday, is the most colourful celebration, particularly in Lamu. Dates vary every year.

Practical Matters

TIME DIFFERENCES

GMT	Kenya	Germany	USA (NY)	Netherlands	Spain
12 noon	3PM	1PM	7AM	1PM	1PM

BEFORE YOU GO

WHAT YOU NEED

- ● Required
- ○ Suggested
- ▲ Not required

	UK	Germany	USA	Netherlands	Spain
Passport	●	●	●	●	●
Visa	▲	▲	●	●	▲
Onward or Return Ticket	●	●	●	●	●
Health Inoculations (➤ 123, Health)	●	●	●	●	●
Health Documentation (➤ 123, Health)	●	●	●	●	●
Travel Insurance	●	●	●	●	●
Driving Licence (national, International recommended)	●	●	●	●	●
Car Insurance Certificate (if own car)	●	●	●	●	●
Car Registration Document (if own car)	●	●	●	●	●

WHEN TO GO

Mombasa (tropical)

High season

Low season

JAN	FEB	MAR	APR	MAY	JUN	JUL	AUG	SEP	OCT	NOV	DEC
High season	High season	Low season	Low season	Low season	High season	High season	High season	High season	Low season	Low season	Low season
32°C	32°C	33°C	31°C	29°C	29°C	28°C	28°C	29°C	30°C	31°C	33°C
Sun	Sun	Sunshine & showers	Very wet	Very wet	Sunshine & showers	Sunshine & showers	Sun	Sun	Sunshine & showers	Wet	Wet

Very wet · Wet · Cloud · Sun · Sunshine & showers

TOURIST OFFICES

In the UK
Kenya National Tourist Office
25 Brook's Mews, Off Davies Street
Mayfair, London WIY ILG
☎ 0171 355 3144
Fax: 0171 495 8656

In the USA
Kenya National Tourist Office
424 Madison Avenue
New York NY 10017
☎ 212/486 1300
Fax: 212)/688 0911

Kenya National Tourist Office
9150 Wilshire Boulevard (60)
Beverly Hills CA 90212
☎ 310/274 6635
Fax: 310/859 7010

POLICE 999

FIRE 999

AMBULANCE 999 (DIRECT DIAL PHONES)

FLYING DOCTOR 501280 (from Nairobi)

WHEN YOU ARE THERE

ARRIVING

Kenya Airways operates direct, daily or weekly flights from most European, Asian and African cities to Nairobi's Jomo Kenyatta airport, or Moi International Airport, Mombasa. A new airport at Eldoret is complete and ready for commissioning. British Airways has scheduled flights to Nairobi, and charter holiday flights fly from London, Gatwick airport.

Jomo Kenyatta Airport, Nairobi

Kilometres to city centre	Journey times	
	🚇	N/A
15 kilometres	🚌	45 minutes
	🚗	20 minutes

Moi International Airport, Mombasa

Kilometres to city centre	Journey times	
	🚇	N/A
13 kilometres	🚌	45 minutes
	🚗	20 minutes

MONEY

The monetary unit of Kenya is the Kenya Shilling (KES or Ksh) divided into 100 cents (cts). There are coins of 5 and 10 cents (bronze) and 50 cents, 1, 5 and 10 shillings (silver). Notes are in denominations of 10, 20, 50, 100, 200, 500 and 1,000 shillings. The 20 shillings note is sometimes referred to as a 'pound note'.

TIME

Kenya is three hours ahead of Greenwich Mean Time (GMT +3).

Kenya is so close to the Equator that all days, throughout the year, are about the same length, around 12 hours of daylight with the sun directly overhead.

CUSTOMS

YES

There are specific allowances of alcohol, cigarettes and luxury goods into the country for those over 16 years of age.

Alcohol: spirits:	1L or
wine:	1L
Cigarettes:	200
Cigars:	50 or
Tobacco:	250 grams
Toilet water:	0.5L

of which not more than 0.125L may be perfume.

Radios, tape recorders, video equipment, photographic equipment, refundable deposits may be required. Gifts will be charged duty.

NO

Agricultural products or pets. Firearms and ammunition may be imported only with a police permit.

EMBASSIES AND CONSULATES

UK	**Germany**	**USA**	**Netherlands**	**Spain**
(02) 335944 (N); (011)	(02) 712527 (N)	(02) 334141 (N)	(02) 581125 (N); (011)	(02) 335711 (N)
312817/472091 (M)	(011) 314732 (M)		311043/315005 (M)	

WHEN YOU ARE THERE

TOURIST OFFICES

- **Nairobi**
  Ministry of Tourism and Wildlife
  Tourist Office
  Utalii House, Uhuru Highway
  PO Box 30027, Nairobi
  ☎ (02) 331030
  Fax: (02) 217604

  Kenya Association of Tour Operators
  Hughes Building
  3rd Floor
  Kenyatta Avenue
  PO Box 48461, Nairobi
  ☎ (02) 225570
  Fax: (02) 218402

- **Mombasa**
  Mombasa Tourist Office
  Jubilee Insurance Building
  Ground Floor – Moi Avenue
  PO Box 80091, Mombasa
  ☎ (011) 223465

  Mombasa and Coast Tourism Association
  Moi Avenue
  PO Box 99596, Mombasa
  ☎ (011) 225428/311231

- **Malindi**
  Malindi Tourist Office
  P O Box 421
  Malindi
  ☎ (0123) 20747

  Travel agencies in the various resorts will also have tourist information.

NATIONAL HOLIDAYS

J	F	M	A	M	J	J	A	S	O	N	D
2	1	1	1	1	1				2		3

1 January	New Year's Day
Jan/Feb	Id ul Fitr (end of Ramadan Celebrations)
Mar/Ap	Good Friday/Easter Monday
1 May	Labour Day
1 June	Madaraka Day
10 Oct	Moi Day
20 Oct	Kenyatta Day
12 Dec	Jamhuri (Independence) Day
25 Dec	Christmas Day
26 Dec	Boxing Day

Holidays falling on a Sunday are observed the following Monday. Muslim festivals are timed according to various phases of the moon and dates vary. During Ramadan, normal business patterns may be interrupted.

OPENING HOURS

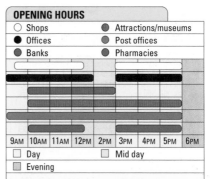

○ Shops	● Attractions/museums
● Offices	● Post offices
● Banks	● Pharmacies

9AM 10AM 11AM 12PM 2PM 3PM 4PM 5PM 6PM

☐ Day   ☐ Mid day
☐ Evening

Banks and post offices have half-day closing on Saturday and shop times may vary in tourist centres.
Opening times of museums are a guide only, times may vary.

**DRIVE ON THE
LEFT**

**TOILETS
BASIC**

**Ask in hotels,
restaurants,
museums and
larger stores**

PUBLIC TRANSPORT

 Internal flights are operated by Kenya Airways, whose network includes scheduled services from Nairobi to Mombasa, Malindi, Lamu Island and Kisumu, as well as inclusive tours to the game parks and coast. For reservations (Nairobi) ☎ (02) 822111. There are also private airlines which operate light aircraft to small air strips. Major companies include Africair, Air Kenya and Prestige Airways.

 Trains Kenya Railways operates a fairly modern, if somewhat limited service. The only routes are: Nairobi– Mombasa; Nairobi–Kisumu; Nairobi–MalabaVoi–Taveta (in south-eastern corner of the country). Travel is in de luxe, second or third-class carriages. All upperclass places should be booked in advance.

 Buses In Kenya the buses are almost entirely the small, brightly painted little Nissan-type matatus, which are, in fact, privately- owned vans. You need either to bargain or ask the cost of the journey when you get in. Drivers tout for business at Nairobi's bus station. On some major roads, such as the very busy, pot-holed Mombasa Nairobi highway you can take bigger and speedier bus transport. Many large hotels offer their own bus services which are sometimes more expensive.

 Ferries These run between Mombasa, Malindi and Lamu. Contact the local tourist office and tour operators for schedules.

CAR RENTAL

To hire a car you must be over 23 and under 70 years, and have held a driving licence for a minimum of two years. It is a good idea to have your passport with you. Shop around, prices can be high. 4-WD is recommended. Check vehicle before a long-distance drive. Foreign driving licences are valid for up to 90 days from arrival, but must be endorsed in Kenya at a local police station.

TAXIS

 These are not hailed, but there are taxi ranks, usually outside hotels and central points **Always ask**, before you get in, how much a journey will be, as there can be extra charges for numbers and luggage, and don't hand over any money before you set off.
It is always wise to take a taxi to a part of town unknown to you, especially after dark.

DRIVING

Speed limit on all country roads (There are no motorways): **62mph (100kph)**

Speed limit in game parks and reserves: **18.5mph (30kph)**

Speed limit on urban roads: **31mph (50kph)**

Must be worn in front seats at all times and in rear seats where fitted.

No laws but police may stop you for random vehicle checks.

Petrol contains ethanol, which can cause problems in the hot weather. It is measured in litres, Premium grade is used in the majority of cars. All towns and villages (except the very smallest) have petrol for sale, but it is wise carry spare water and fuel in cans if driving in remote areas.

Most reputable car hire firms are members of the Automobile Association of Kenya (AAK), Tel: (02) 720382 (Nairobi) who have patrols on the major highways, while in the parks nearly all lodges have resident mechanics. In the event of breakdown phone the car rental company, who will deal with the situation.

CENTIMETRES

INCHES

PERSONAL SAFETY

Kenya's police force is renowned for its efficiency, and treat very seriously any offences against Foreign Exchange Control, sexual and drug abuse, traffic regulations and prostitution. Great care should be taken if driving in game parks. It is advisable to hire a professional guide.

To avoid danger or theft:

- At the airport, do not leave items unguarded, especially cameras and new luggage.

- Leave money and valuables in the hotel safe. Carry only the minimum with you and keep it hidden.

- Do not walk alone at night or down approach roads to beaches.

- Do not drive out of the city at night as breakdown services will not come out after dark.

- When in game parks, do not leave your vehicle. Wild animals are dangerous, but will not attack vehicles.

- Do not bathe in stagnant or river water.

Police assistance:
☎ **999**
from any call box

TELEPHONES

There is a good service within the country but not too many telephones. Payphones, often awkward to operate, take KES 3 for local calls. Most major towns are covered by the direct-dial system. The code for Nairobi is 02. For enquiries dial 991. Cardphones are best for international calls. (They do not take ordinary credit cards.)

International dialling codes:

From Kenya to:	
UK	001 44
Germany	001 37
USA and Canada	001 1
Netherlands	001 31
Spain	001 34
Australia	001 61
New Zealand	001 64

POST

For receiving mail, *post restante* is a free service at larger post offices. When posting home, stamps can be bought only at post offices and larger hotels. All towns have main post offices and there are sub-post offices in rural areas, except in the far north of the country. Most hotels operate a postal service for their guests.

ELECTRICITY

The power supply is: 240 volts, 50 cycles AC

 Type of socket: Square three-pin

The plugs used are the same as in Britain. Other visitors should bring an adaptor for their 110 volt 60 cycle plugs 110-volt razor points are usually available in larger hotels and lodges.

TIPS/GRATUITIES

Yes ✓ No ✗		
Restaurants (service included, tip optional)	✗	
Bar service	✓	10%
Taxis (negotiate price first, tip optional)	✗	
Tour guides, especially on safari per day	✓	Ksh 100–200
Drivers	✓	Ksh 100–200
Porters	✓	Ksh 50–100
Hairdressers	✓	Ksh 50–100

PHOTOGRAPHY

What to photograph: A telephoto lens is essential for photographing the wildlife. The best time for the light is in the early morning or late afternoon
Where you need permission to photograph: Kenyans do not like to be photographed without permission and possibly payment. Do not try to photograph the President or at airports, harbours and any police or military buildings.
Where to buy film: Film is available in many shops but take what you need with you, particularly colour transparency film or black and white.

HEALTH

Insurance

Medical insurance is essential; medical treatment in East Africa is not free and public hospitals very crowded. Be certain that you are covered for repatriation or any time necessary in hospital. No reciprocal agreements exist.

Dental Services

Have a thorough dental check-up before leaving home. Dentists are few and far between in Africa and treatment is expensive. Medical insurance is advisable.

Sun Advice

Kenya is on the Equator and the sun is immediately overhead all year round. It is easy to burn and get sunstroke, even in the shade. Always wear a hat and sunglasses, drink plenty of fluids and wear a high-protection sunscreen.

Drugs

Pharmacies dispensing prescription and over the counter treatments are in major centres. Anti-malaria tablets should be taken before, during and after your visit. Anti-diarrhoea tablets are advisable. Visitors requiring special or continued medication should bring sufficient to cover the duration of their stay. It is also advisable to bring a first-aid kit.

A yellow fever vaccination certificate is required for travellers from endemic areas. Although a cholera certificate is not now required, up-to-date advice should be sought regarding vaccination.

Safe Water

Drinking unboiled local water can cause acute stomach problems. Use bottled water and do not eat uncooked food, especially salads washed in local water. Avoid ice in drinks.

CONCESSIONS

Students/Youths A student card (ISIC) will obtain a fifty-percent reduction on entrance fees to most of the National parks and game reserves
Senior Citizens Discounts are sometimes available at coastal resorts, on boat trips etc. You may have to negotiate and may need your passport.
As with almost everything in Kenya, price concessions are open to negotiation and bargaining.

CLOTHING SIZES

NB
In Kenya
S = Small
M = Medium
L = Large

Kenya	UK	Rest of Europe	USA	
36	36	46	36	Suits
38	38	48	38	
40	40	50	40	
42	42	52	42	
44	44	54	44	
46	46	56	46	
7	7	41	8	Shoes
7.5	7.5	42	8.5	
8.5	8.5	43	9.5	
9.5	9.5	44	10.5	
10.5	10.5	45	11.5	
11	11	46	12	
S	14.5	37	14.5	Shirts
S	15	38	15	
M	15.5	39/40	15.5	
M	16	41	16	
L	16.5	42	16.5	
L	17	43	17	
S	8	34	6	Dresses
S	10	36	8	
S	12	38	10	
M	14	40	12	
M	16	42	14	
L	18	44	16	
4.5	4.5	37.5	6	Shoes
5	5	38	6.5	
5.5	5.5	38.5	7	
6	6	39	7.5	
6.5	6.5	40	8	
7	7	41	8.5	

WHEN DEPARTING

- An airport departure tax equivalent to US$20, is payable in foreign currency or in Ksh for international flights; for domestic flights the fee is Ksh100. Remaining Kenyan currency should be converted to a foreign currency before departure.
- Arrive at the airport at least two hours before departure.
- If you are crossing to a neighbouring country, check you have all the necessary papers and inoculations.

LANGUAGE

In common with many other African states. Kenya has a number of tribal tongues, it is however, only Swahili that you will need, other than English, which is extensively understood in the cities and the tourist areas. It is not difficult to learn a few words and pronunciation is easy – every letter is sounded fully except ch and sh, which are as in English.

Below is a list of a few words that may be helpful.

guest house	nyumba yo wageni	washing water	maji yo kuosha
room/s	chumba/vyumba	can I stay here?	naweza kukaa hapa
bed/s	banda	how much?	ngapi?
small dwelling	kitanda/vitanda	Is there any...?	Iko...? or Kuna...?
toilet	choo	No there isn't any	Haiko... or Hakuna...
bathroom	bafu	Yes there is...	Iko... or Kuna...
hot/cold water	maji/moto/baridi	sleep	lala

bank	benki	fixed price	bei moha
post office	posta	expensive	ghali sana
How much?	Ngapi?	Reduce the price, come down a little	Punguza kidogo
money	pesa		
What price?	Bei gani?		
fifty cents	sumni	tip, bribe	'chai'

small restaurant (not hotel)	hoteli	meat	nyama
table	meza	roast meat	nyama choma
tea (black)	chai (kavu)	vegetables	mboga
coffee	kahawa	fruit	matunda
beer	bia	chicken	kuku
water	maji or mai	hot	moto
bill	hesabu	cold	baridi
bread	mkate	bananas	ndizi
fish	samaki	rice	mchele or wali
		maize meal	posho

bus/es	bas, basi/mabasi	The car has broken down	Gari inevunjika
car/s	gari/magari	When does it leave?	Inaondoka lini?
taxi	teksi		
train	treni		
aeroplane	ndege	Where are you going?	Unaeunda Wapi
boat/ship	chombo/meli		
petrol	petroli	I want to go to...	mimi nataka kwenda...
Stop!	Simama!		

Hello	Jambo or Habari	child	mtoto
		Goodbye	kwaheri
yes	ndiyo	doctor	daktari
no	hapana	I'm ill	Mimi mgonjwa
Thank you	Asante	police	polisi
Mister... (Monsieur...)	Bwana...	today	leo
		tomorrow	kesho
Mrs...(Madame..)	Mama	My name is	Jina langu...

INDEX

Acknowledgements
The Automobile Association wishes to thank the following photographers and libraries for their assistance in the preparation of this book.

JAMES DEAN TRAVEL PHOTOGRAPHY F/cover: Masai woman
MARY EVANS PICTURE LIBRARY 10b
MRI BANKERS' GUIDE TO FOREIGN CURRENCY 119
PAUL MURPHY 25b, 26b, 44b, 68b
PICTURES COLOUR LIBRARY F/cover: Amboseli National Park
MELISSA SHALES 19b, 40b, 41b, 65b, 72b
ZEFA PICTURES LTD 76b
The remaining photographs are held in the Association's own library (AA PHOTO LIBRARY) and were taken by Paul Kenward with the exception of the following pages: 1, 2, 14b, 17b, 28b, 33, 36b, 37b, 51a, 54b, 56, 58b, 66b, 71, 72a, 73a, 74a, 75a, 76a, 77a, 77b, 78, 79a, 79b, 80a, 91a, 92, 93, 94, 95, 96, 97, 98, 99, 100, 101, 102, 103, 104, 105, 106, 107, 108, 109, 110, 111, 112, 113, 114, 115, 116 which were taken by Eric Meacher; and F/cover: lions, and B/cover: coffee beans taken by Clive Sawyer.

Author's Acknowledgements
Paul Murphy would like to thank James Taylour-Sullivan, Sarova Hotels; Michael Fowler, Lonrho Hotels; Chris Flatt, Bush Homes; John and Barbara Barton, Ololerai Farm; Tony, Adrianne and Robert Mills, Lokitela Farm; John and Lulu Clark, Diani House; Dick and Rosemary Knight, Sable Valley; Alastair Addison, Hemingway's; Alex Miller, Musiara; George, Governor's Camp; Mara Balloon Safaris; Zul Dhanji, Hertz; Wasini Island Restaurant and Kisite Dhow Tours; Abdul Lodhi, Yumbe House/Yumbe Villas. Thanks also to John Glenn and Leonard Kiragu, UTC; Bill Adams, Safari Consultants, Kenya Airways and Kenya Wildlife Service.

Contributors
Copy editor: Karen Bird   Page Layout: Phil Barfoot   Verifier: Polly Phillimore
Researcher (Practical Matters): Lesley Allard   Indexer: Marie Lorimer